In praise of the Blasing/Konuk translations of Nazim Hikmet:

"I would like to see Hikmet's work have a wide audience here and become—as it may—a profound influence on American poets." —DENISE LEVERTOV

"These are many of the most overwhelming poems in English." —STEPHEN BERG

"Such a poet as Hikmet is beyond our hopes in this country." —DAVID IGNATOW

"Many of these are a real addition to contemporary poetry in English." —W.S. MERWIN

"Brilliantly conceived and executed, witty and passionate, and inspiring in a sense not found in most modern poems." —*Booklist*

"These poems have range and power; they speak directly to the reader despite differences in background or politics." —*Library Journal*

"Lucid, colloquial, vivid English." —*Los Angeles Times*

"Lively and readable." —DON SHEWEY, *The Village Voice*

"These translations are so colloquial one forgets one isn't reading the originals." —KEN EMERSON, *The Boston Phoenix*

"Hikmet speaks in these translations as a contemporary." —JOHN BRADLEY, *The Bloomsbury Review*

"This poetry electrifies me—I weep when I read it, my skin tingles." —JONATHAN CHAVES, *Montemora*

"A potent testament to the Turkish poet's genius." —TALAT SAIT HALMAN, *World Literature Today*

POEMS OF NAZIM HIKMET

Revised and Expanded

Translated from the Turkish by
RANDY BLASING & MUTLU KONUK

Foreword by
CAROLYN FORCHÉ

A Karen and Michael Braziller Book
PERSEA BOOKS / NEW YORK

Grateful acknowledgment is made to the editors of the magazines in which many of these translations originally appeared: *The American Poetry Review, The Antioch Review, Ararat, The Denver Quarterly, The Literary Review, Literature East & West, Persea, Poetry East, Poetry Now,* and *Translation.*

Requests for permission to reprint or make photocopies and for any other information should be addressed to the publisher:

Persea Books
853 Broadway
New York, New York 10003

Library of Congress Cataloging-in-Publication Data

Nazim Hikmet, 1902–1963.
    [Poems. English. Selections]
    Poems of Nazim Hikmet / translated from the Turkish by Randy Blasing & Mutlu Konuk.—Rev. & expanded.
      p. cm.
  ISBN 0-89255-274-3 (pbk : alk. paper)
    I. Blasing, Randy. II. Blasing, Mutlu Konuk, 1944– III. Title.

PL248.H45 A6 2002
894'.3513—dc21   2001059118

Manufactured in the United States of America
Second Edition

CONTENTS

TRANSLATORS' PREFACE

THIS SECOND EDITION of *Poems of Nazim Hikmet* contains the hundred poems that we consider his best both in Turkish and in translation. The culmination of thirty-five years of trying to give voice to Hikmet in English, it expands the first edition (1994) by adding twenty-one poems and includes more than twenty others that have been significantly revised. Spanning his career—from early, in-your-face Futurist experiments to late, headlong explorations of personal memory; from expansive, crypto-factual historical narratives to crystalline, near-mystical love lyrics; from free verse to traditional forms—these versions are meant to reflect the range as well as the quality of his achievement.

As always, we are grateful to Karen and Michael Braziller of Persea Books for bringing Hikmet to the attention of the English-speaking world; for more than a quarter-century they have made our labor of love their own.

R.B.
M.K.
September 2001
Çeşme, Turkey-Providence, Rhode Island

FOREWORD

IF ONE DISCOVERS a poet in a felicitous hour—in the wakefulness of convalescence, in a crisis of spirit, or in a moment of uncommon suffering or joy—that poet becomes for the reader a tutelary spirit. Such was my encounter with the poetry of Nazim Hikmet, twenty-four years ago on a winter afternoon in the apartment of a young poet in upstate New York. "Read this," the poet said, pressing the book into my hands as I have proffered it to countless others since, "you really must." We stood at the window, reading by its light as the snow fell, and Hikmet's poetry became for me a species of guidebook, a manual for living, advising one to embrace what came to pass, to say *yes,* to live fully, and, most daunting, to be able to *die for people—/even for people whose faces you've never seen.*

From the tradition of Lucretius' *De rerum natura* and Virgil's *Georgics,* Hikmet rescued the didactic mode for a modern Turkish poetry of epic breadth and lyric grace, benefiting those who would survive imprisonment, struggle, and exile in the twentieth century. If, as the French Resistance poet Robert Desnos has written, *the earth is a camp lit by thousands of spiritual fires,* Hikmet is among them; if it is true, as Bertolt Brecht believed, that *the world's one hope* lies in *the compassion of the oppressed for the oppressed,* then Hikmet serves as an exemplar of that hope. With the work of César Vallejo, Pablo Neruda, Rafael Alberti, Yannis Ritsos, Attila József, George Oppen, and Mahmoud Darwish, Hikmet's poetry is marked by the impress of extremity and a faith in the salvific possibility of global fraternity and social justice, preserving the intensely personal subjectivity of a lyric selfhood that finds within the self a capacity for filiation.

Such concerns, joined to the praxis of Marxism, are anathematized as destructive of poetic art, and so we are a bit startled to discover in Hikmet an engagée poet writing poignantly and prophetically, seemingly without ideological encumbrance. His fellow Marxist the Italian theorist Antonio Gramsci wrote from prison: "How many times have I asked myself whether it was possible to tie oneself to a mass without ever having loved anyone . . . whether one could love a collectivity if one hadn't deeply loved some single human beings."[1] This regard for love, *eros* and *agape*, suffuses Hikmet's lyric art and informs his own criticism of "certain people who pass for 'leftists' " but who separate mind and heart.

For his own political views, Hikmet spent thirteen years in prison and thirteen in exile; he is one of the twentieth century's strongest voices of the carceral imagination and exilic being. In the darkness of our time, these have become sub-genres of literary art. Yet under Hikmet's pen the carceral silence of solitary confinement becomes an intimate prosopopoeia (his interlocutor a longed-for but absent wife) and exilic displacement a borderless country where one encounters *the most honest people on earth—/I mean, affectionate like violins, /pitiless and brave/like children who can't talk yet, /ready to die as easily as birds /or live a thousand years.* In the former, he chronicles his experience of confinement in carceral space with the precision of a cartographer and a genius for guilelessness and the articulation of raw emotion. He sounds the depths of the personal to determine its significance while voicing the struggle to preserve his inner equilibrium and, hence, his humanity in the midst of degradation. What remains past suffering is his capacity to be moved by flickering apprehensions of natural phenomena: *chestnut leaves . . . falling on boulevards, the tongue of a leopard at a spring.*

In prison as well as in exile, he is in love with *earth, light, struggle, bread,* but also with *song, tobacco, hazelnuts, Amasya apples, eggs and bulgur, gilded purple eggplants, the color of pomegranate seeds, melons fragrant, plums tart, the smell of geranium leaves on my fingers.* These litanies of abundance in a sensorium real or imagined attest to the poet's keen specificity of diction, as well as a sensibility inclined toward phenomenological celebration. He is in love with life in its fecundity, complexity, beauty, and horror; to live, for him, is a *solemn duty,* and he excoriates himself for fleeting moments of self-pity. He cautions those who will serve time in prison against the languor of nostalgia, advising a vigilance against lice and the contemplation of *seas and mountains* rather than *roses and gardens*. He advises laughter, weaving, the making of mirrors, and reminds us *always remember / to eat every last piece of bread*, and that *a prisoner's wife* should buy him *flannel underwear* and *must always think good thoughts*. These are practical matters, lessons from excruciating experience. Above all, he cautions, one's heart and one's love must be preserved. He dismisses his own pain with an off-handed "and so on" or "etcetera": *And anything else, / such as my ten years here, / is just so much talk.*

What is most interesting about these carceral and exilic poems is their recourse to the journey, real or imagined, and poetic devices associated with inscribing speed, motion, and movement through space and time. He is, remarkably for his era, a poet of the synchronic imagination—*Who knows at this very moment / which drunk is killing his wife? / Who knows at this very moment / which ghost . . . / Who knows at this very moment / which thief*—and also of cinematographic technique: the pan, the dissolve, the cut. The poem is in motion, as written from a train window or cabin porthole. Dream and waking are interspliced, as are past and present. Hikmet apprehends the universe as *blue vacancies / full of glittering discs,* and we view Africa from space as *a huge violin*. Time, and its experience as duration, collapse. *I had a pencil / the year I was thrown inside. / It lasted me a week. / If you ask it: / "A whole lifetime!" / If you ask me: / "What's a week?"* To his wife, he writes: *in the twentieth century / grief lasts / at most a year.* From exile he longs for *just one hour in Istanbul*. But his journeys are epic, not only in his recounting of the life and death of Sheik Bedreddin but in many other poems, especially "Straw-Blond," his missive to his beloved Russian wife, Vera, which takes us in visionary sequences through Warsaw, Prague, Berlin, Moscow, Paris, then Havana, and Paris again. From his cell he takes flight to join *the workers in Adana / or in the Greek mountains or in China,* and if he suffers in prison from angina, his heart is also *with the army flowing / toward the Yellow River. / And every morning at sunrise my heart / is shot in Greece.* He drifts between dream and waking consciousness, suffering and delusion, flights of imagination and dissolution of self.

Regarded as the most revolutionary Turkish poet since Fuzuli seven hundred years earlier, Hikmet fused indigenous folk poetry and classical, Persian-influenced court poetry into a colloquial, modified free verse of highly varied meters and irregular rhymes, producing intimate epistolary monologues, poetic diaries, lyric epics, polyphonic conversations, and a fanciful ekphrastic poem on the love between the *Mona Lisa* (his "Gioconda") and a Chinese revolutionary, Si-Ya-U. Hikmet's language is a speaking-forth, an utterance in a symphony of the silenced, invoking the spirits of tailor, iron-caster, shepherd, fruit peddler, ironworker, typesetter, papermaker, blue-shirted builder, *painters of Seljuk china, weavers of fiery rugs,* gem cutters, Bornese cabin boys, *naked coolies* sorting rice, and tinsmiths. Whether he is writing from prison, from hotel rooms, balconies, or trains, from the skies over Africa, from the sea between Leningrad and Stockholm or the China and Arabian seas, or from the moment of watching a woman *wash the lice from her dirty shirt* to the hour when he writes *I carved your name on my watchband / with my fingernail,* we are in the presence of a rare guide to the work of remaining hopeful and in love with life, pure of heart and human, passionate and dedicated to the common good.

Carolyn Forché

---

[1]Antonio Gramsci, *Selections from the Prison Notebooks* (London: Lawrence and Wishart, 1971), p. 87.

INTRODUCTION

NAZIM HIKMET, popularly recognized and critically acclaimed in Turkey as the first and foremost modern Turkish poet, is known around the world as one of the great international poets of the twentieth century, and his poetry has been translated into more than fifty languages. Born in 1902 in Salonika, where his father was in the foreign service, Hikmet grew up in Istanbul. His mother was an artist, and his pasha grandfather wrote poetry; through their circle of friends Hikmet was introduced to poetry early, publishing his first poems at seventeen. He attended the Turkish naval academy, but during the Allied occupation of Istanbul following the First World War, he left to teach in eastern Turkey.

In 1922, after a brief first marriage ended in annulment, he crossed the border and made his way to Moscow, attracted by the Russian Revolution and its promise of social justice. At Moscow University he got to know students and artists from all over the world. He returned to Turkey in 1924, after the Turkish War of Independence, but soon was arrested for working on a leftist magazine. In 1926 he managed to escape to Russia, where he remarried, met Mayakovsky, and worked in the theater with Meyerhold.

A general amnesty allowed Hikmet to return to Turkey in 1928. Since the Communist Party had been outlawed by then, he found himself under constant surveillance by the secret police and spent five of the next ten years in prison on a variety of trumped-up charges. In 1933, for example, he was jailed for putting up illegal posters, but when his case came to trial, it was thrown out of court for lack of evidence. Meanwhile, between 1929 and 1936 he published nine books—five collections and four long poems—that revolutionized Turkish poetry, flouting Ottoman literary conventions and introducing free verse and colloquial diction. While these poems established him as a new major poet, he also published several plays and novels and worked as a bookbinder, proofreader, journalist, translator, and screen-writer to support an extended family that included his third wife, two stepchildren, and widowed mother.

Then in January 1938 he was arrested for inciting the Turkish armed forces to revolt and sentenced to twenty-eight years in prison on the grounds that military cadets were reading his poems, particularly *The Epic of Sheik Bedreddin*. Published in 1936, this long poem based on a fifteenth-century peasant rebellion against Ottoman rule was his last book to appear in Turkey during his lifetime. His friend Pablo Neruda relates Hikmet's account of how he was treated after his arrest: "Accused of attempting to incite the Turkish navy into rebellion, Nazim was condemned to the punishments of hell. The trial was held on a warship. He told me he was forced to walk on the ship's bridge until he was too weak to stay on his feet, then they stuck him into a section of the latrines where the excrement rose half a meter above the floor. My brother poet felt his strength failing him. The stench made him reel. Then the thought struck him: my tormentors are keeping an eye on me, they want to see me drop, they want to watch me suffer. His strength came back with pride. He began to sing, low at first, then louder, and finally at the top of his lungs. He sang all the songs, all the love poems he could re-member, his own poems, the ballads of the peasants, the people's battle hymns. He sang everything he knew. And so he vanquished the filth and his torturers."*

In prison, Hikmet's Futurist-inspired, often topical early poetry gave way to poems with a more direct manner and a more serious tone. Enclosed in letters to his family and friends, they were subsequently circulated in manuscript. He not only com-posed some of his greatest lyrics in prison but produced, between 1941 and 1945, his epic masterwork, *Human Landscapes*. He also learned such crafts as weaving and woodworking in order to

---

Memoirs, trans. Hardie St. Martin (New York: Penguin, 1978), pp. 195–96.

support himself and his family. In the late Forties, while still in prison, he divorced his third wife and married for the fourth time. In 1949 an international committee, including Pablo Picasso, Paul Robeson, and Jean-Paul Sartre, was formed in Paris to campaign for Hikmet's release, and in 1950 he was awarded the World Peace Prize. The same year, he went on an eighteen-day hunger strike, despite a recent heart attack, and when Turkey's first democratically elected government came to power, he was released in a general amnesty.

Within a year, however, his persecution had resumed full force. Simone de Beauvoir recalls him describing the events of that time: "He told me how a year after he came out of prison there were two attempts to murder him (with cars, in the narrow streets of Istanbul). And then they tried to make him do military service on the Russian frontier: he was fifty. The doctor, a major, said to him: 'Half an hour standing in the sun and you're a dead man. But I shall have to give you a certificate of health.' So then he escaped, across the Bosporus in a tiny motorboat on a stormy night—when it was calm the straits were too well guarded. He wanted to reach Bulgaria, but it was impossible with a high sea running. He passed a Rumanian cargo ship, he began to circle it, shouting his name. They saluted him, they waved handkerchiefs, but they didn't stop. He followed and went on circling them in the height of the storm; after two hours they stopped, but without picking him up. His motor stalled, he thought he was done for. At last they hauled him aboard; they had been telephoning to Bucharest for instructions. Exhausted, half dead, he staggered into the officers' cabin; there was an enormous photograph of him with the caption: SAVE NAZIM HIKMET. The most ironical part, he added, was that he had already been at liberty for over a year."*

---

*Force of Circumstance, trans. Richard Howard (New York: Putnam's, 1965), pp. 390–91.

Taken to Moscow, he was given a house in the writers' colony of Peredelkino outside the city; the Turkish government denied his wife and infant son permission to join him. Although he suffered a second heart attack in 1952, Hikmet traveled widely during his exile, visiting not only Eastern Europe but Rome, Paris, Havana, Peking, and Tanganyika: "I traveled through Europe, Asia, and Africa with my dream / only the Americans didn't give me visa." Stripped of his Turkish citizenship in 1959, he chose to become a citizen of Poland, explaining he had inherited his blue eyes and red hair from a Polish ancestor who was a seventeenth-century revolutionary. In 1959 he also married again. The increasingly breathless pace of his late poems—often unpunctuated and, toward the end, impatient even with line divisions—conveys a sense of time accelerating as he grows older and travels faster and farther than ever before in his life. During his exile his poems were regularly printed abroad, his *Selected Poems* was published in Bulgaria in 1954, and generous translations of his work subsequently appeared there and in Greece, Germany, Italy, and the USSR. He died of a heart attack in Moscow in June 1963.

After his death, Hikmet's books began to reappear in Turkey; in 1965 and 1966, for example, more than twenty of his books were published there, some of them reprints of earlier volumes and others works appearing for the first time. The next fifteen years saw the gradual publication of his eight-volume *Collected Poems*, along with his plays, novels, letters, and children's stories. At the same time, various selections of his poems went through multiple printings, and numerous biographies and critical studies of his poetry were published. Since his death, major translations of his poetry have continued to appear in England, France, Germany, Greece, Poland, Spain, and the United States; for example, Yannis Ritsos's Greek versions had gone through eight printings as of 1977, and Philippe Soupault's 1964 "anthology" was reissued in France as recently as 1982. And in 1983 alone, new translations of Hikmet's poems were published in French, German, and Russian.

Like Whitman, Hikmet speaks of himself, his country, and the world in the same breath. "I want to write poems," he is reported saying, "that both talk only about me and address just one other person and call out to millions. I want to write poems that talk of a single apple, of the plowed earth, of the psyche of someone getting out of prison, of the struggle of the masses for a better life, of one man's heartbreaks. I want to write poems about both fearing and not fearing death." At once personal and public, his poetry records his life without reducing it to self-consciousness; he affirms the reality of facts at the same time that he insists on the validity of his feelings. His human presence or the controlling figure of his personality—playful, optimistic, and capable of childlike joy—keeps his poems open, public, and committed to social and artistic change.

In the perfect oneness of his life and art, Hikmet emerges as a heroic figure. His early poems proclaim this unity as a faith: art is an event, he maintains, in social as well as literary history, and a poet's bearing in art is inseparable from his bearing in life. The rest of Hikmet's life gave him ample opportunity to act upon this faith and, in fact, to deepen it. As Terrence Des Pres observes, Hikmet's "exemplary life" and "special vision"—"at once historical and timeless, Marxist *and* mystical"—had unique consequences for his art: "Simply because in his art and in his person Hikmet opposes the enemies of the human spirit in harmony with itself and the earth, he can speak casually and yet with a seriousness that most modern American poets never dream of attempting."* In a sense, Hikmet's prosecutors honored him by believing a book of poems could incite the military to revolt; indeed, the fact that he was persecuted attests to the credibility of his belief in the vital importance of his art. Yet the suffering his faith cost him—he never compromised in his life or art—is

---

*"Poetry and Politics: The Example of Nazim Hikmet," *Parnassus* 6 (Spring/Summer 1978): 12, 23.

only secondary to the suffering that must have gone into keeping that faith. The circumstances of his life are very much to the point, not only because he continually chose to remain faithful to his vision, but also because his life and art form a dramatic whole. Sartre remarked that Hikmet conceived of a human being as something to be created. In his life no less than in his art, Hikmet forged this new kind of person, who was heroic by virtue of being a creator. This conception of the artist as a hero and of the hero as a creator saves art from becoming a frivolous activity in the modern world; as Hikmet's career dramatizes, poetry is a matter of life and death.

Mutlu Konuk

Poems of Nazim Hikmet

ABOUT MY POETRY

I have no silver-saddled horse to ride,
no inheritance to live on,
neither riches nor real estate—
a pot of honey is all I own.
A pot of honey
                    red as fire!

My honey is my everything.
I guard
my riches and my real estate
—my honey pot, I mean—
from pests of every species.
Brother, just wait...
As long as I've got
honey in my pot,
bees will come to it
                    from Timbuktu...

REGARDING ART

Sometimes I, too, tell the ah's
of my heart one by one
like the blood-red beads
of a ruby rosary strung
      on strands of golden hair!
But my
poetry's muse
takes to the air
on wings made of steel
like the I-beams
      of my suspension bridges!

I don't pretend
      the nightingale's lament
to the rose isn't easy on the ears...
But the language
      that really speaks to me
are Beethoven sonatas played
on copper, iron, wood, bone, and catgut...

You can *have*
galloping off
in a cloud of dust!
Me, I wouldn't trade
for the purest-bred
      Arabian steed
the sixty mph
      of my iron horse
         running on iron tracks!

Sometimes my eye is caught like a big dumb fly
by the masterly spider webs in the corners of my room.
But I really look up

to the seventy-seven-story, reinforced-concrete mountains
my blue-shirted builders create!

Were I to meet
the male beauty
"young Adonis, god of Byblos,"
on a bridge, I'd probably never notice;
but I can't help staring into my philosopher's glassy eyes
or my fireman's square face
red as a sweating sun!

Though I can smoke
third-class cigarettes filled
on my electric workbenches,
I can't roll tobacco—even the finest—
in paper by hand and smoke it!
I didn't—
wouldn't—trade
my wife dressed in her leather cap and jacket
for Eve's nakedness!
Maybe I don't have a "poetic soul"?
What can I do
when I love my own children
more
than Mother Nature's!

GIOCONDA AND SI-YA-U

to the memory of my friend SI-YA-U,
whose head was cut off in Shanghai

A CLAIM

Renowned Leonardo's
world-famous
"La Gioconda"
has disappeared.
And in the space
vacated by the fugitive
a copy has been placed.

The poet inscribing
the present treatise
knows more than a little
about the fate
of the real Gioconda.
She fell in love
with a seductive
graceful youth:
a honey-tongued
almond-eyed Chinese
named SI-YA-U.
Gioconda ran off
after her lover;
Gioconda was burned
in a Chinese city.

I, Nazim Hikmet,
authority
on this matter,
thumbing my nose at friend and foe

five times a day,
undaunted,
claim
I can prove it;
if I can't,
I'll be ruined and banished
forever from the realm of poesy.

1928

Part One
Excerpts from Gioconda's Diary

15 March 1924: Paris, Louvre Museum

At last I am bored with the Louvre Museum.
You get fed up with boredom very fast.
I am fed up with my boredom.
And from the devastation inside me
   I drew this lesson:
     to visit
      a museum is fine,
       to be a museum piece is terrible!
In this palace that imprisons the past
I am placed under such a heavy sentence
that as the paint on my face cracks out of boredom
I'm forced to keep grinning without letting up.
Because
   I am the Gioconda from Florence
whose smile is more famous than Florence.
I am bored with the Louvre Museum.
And since you get sick soon enough
      of conversing with the past,
I decided
   from now on
to keep a diary.
Writing of today may be of some help
      in forgetting yesterday...
However, the Louvre is a strange place.
Here you might find
Alexander the Great's
   Longines watch complete with chronometer,
but
not a single sheet of clean notebook paper

or a pencil worth a piaster.
Damn your Louvre, your Paris.
I'll write these entries
            on the back of my canvas.
And so
when I picked a pen from the pocket
of a nearsighted American
            sticking his red nose into my skirts
—his hair stinking of wine—
                        I started my memoirs.
I'm writing on my back
        the sorrows of having a famous smile . . .

18 March: Night

The Louvre has fallen asleep.
In the dark, the armless Venus
                looks like a veteran of the Great War.
The gold helmet of a knight gleams
as the light from a night watchman's lantern
                        strikes a dark picture.
Here
        in the Louvre
                my days are all the same
                        like the six sides of a wood cube.
My head is full of sharp smells
        like the shelf of a medicine cabinet.

20 March

I admire those Flemish painters:
is it easy to give the air of a naked goddess
                        to the plump ladies

of milk and sausage merchants?
But
        even if you wear silk panties,
cow + silk panties = cow.

Last night
        a window
            was left open.
The naked Flemish goddesses caught cold.
All day
today,
        turning their bare
mountain-like pink behinds to the public,
                            they coughed and sneezed ...
I caught cold, too.
So as not to look silly smiling with a cold,
I tried to hide my sniffles
                    from the visitors.

1 April

Today I saw a Chinese:
        he was nothing like those Chinese with their topknots.
How long
        he gazed at me!
I'm well aware
        the favor of Chinese
                who work ivory like silk
                        is not to be taken lightly ...

11 April

I caught the name of the Chinese who comes every day:
                            SI-YA-U.

16 April

Today we spoke
in the language of eyes.
He works as a weaver days
and studies nights.
Now it's a long time since the night
came on like a pack of black-shirted Fascists.
The cry of a man out of work
who jumped into the Seine
rose from the dark water.
And ah! you on whose fist-size head
                    mountain-like winds descend,
at this very minute you're probably busy
building towers of thick, leather-bound books
to get answers to the questions you asked of the stars.
READ
SI-YA-U
        READ...
And when your eyes find in the lines what they desire,
                            when your eyes tire,
rest your tired head
            like a black-and-yellow Japanese chrysanthemum
                            on the books...
                            SLEEP
                                SI-YA-U
                                    SLEEP...

18 April

I've begun to forget
the names of those fat Renaissance masters.

I want to see
　　　the black bird-and-flower
　　　　　　　　watercolors
　　　　　　that slant-eyed Chinese painters
　　　　　　　　　　　　　drip
　　　　　　from their long thin bamboo brushes.

NEWS FROM THE PARIS WIRELESS

　　　HALLO
　　　　　　HALLO
　　　　　　　　　HALLO
　　　PARIS
　　　　　　PARIS
　　　　　　　　　PARIS...
Voices race through the air
　　　　　　　like fiery greyhounds.
The wireless in the Eiffel Tower calls out:
　　　HALLO
　　　　　　HALLO
　　　　　　　　　HALLO
　　　PARIS
　　　　　　PARIS
　　　　　　　　　PARIS...

"I, TOO, am Oriental—this voice is for me.
My ears are receivers, too.
I, too, must listen to Eiffel."
News from China
　　　　　　News from China
　　　　　　　　　　News from China:
The dragon that came down from the Kaf Mountains
　　　　　　　　　　has spread his wings
across the golden skies of the Chinese homeland.
But
in this business it's not only the British lord's

gullet shaved
      like the thick neck
            of a plucked hen
that will be cut
but also
     the long
        thin
           beard of Confucius!

FROM GIOCONDA'S DIARY

21 April

Today my Chinese
        looked me straight
              in the eye
and asked:
"Those who crush our rice fields
     with the caterpillar treads of their tanks
and who swagger through our cities
     like emperors of hell,
are they of YOUR race,
     the race of him who CREATED you?"
I almost raised my hand
     and cried "No!"

27 April

    Tonight at the blare of an American trumpet
—the horn of a 12-horsepower Ford—
              I awoke from a dream,
and what I glimpsed for an instant
             instantly vanished.
What I'd seen was a still blue lake.

In this lake the slant-eyed light of my life
    had wrapped his fingers around the neck of a gilded fish.
I tried to reach him,
my boat a Chinese teacup
and my sail
        the embroidered silk
                of a Japanese
                    bamboo umbrella . . .

NEWS FROM THE PARIS WIRELESS

        HALLO
            HALLO
                HALLO
    PARIS
        PARIS
            PARIS
The radio station signs off.
Once more
            blue-shirted Parisians
                    fill Paris with red voices
                    and red colors . . .

FROM GIOCONDA'S DIARY

2 May

Today my Chinese failed to show up.

5 May

Still no sign of him . . .

8 May

My days
          are like the waiting room
                         of a station:
eyes glued
          to the tracks . . .

10 May

Sculptors of Greece,
painters of Seljuk china,
weavers of fiery rugs in Persia,
chanters of hymns to dromedaries in deserts,
dancer whose body undulates like a breeze,
craftsman who cuts thirty-six facets from a one-carat stone,
and YOU
          who have five talents on your five fingers,
                    master MICHELANGELO!
Call out and announce to both friend and foe:
because he made too much noise in Paris,
because he smashed in the window
                    of the Mandarin ambassador,
     Gioconda's lover
                    has been thrown out
                              of France . . .
My lover from China has gone back to China . . .
And now I'd like to know
who's Romeo and Juliet!
If he isn't Juliet in pants
                    and I'm not Romeo in skirts . . .
Ah, if I could cry—
                    if only I could cry . . .

12 May

Today
        when I caught a glimpse of myself
           in the mirror of some mother's daughter
touching up the paint
           on her bloody mouth
    in front of me,
    the tin crown of my fame shattered on my head.
While the desire to cry writhes inside me
                I smile demurely;
like a stuffed pig's head
           my ugly face grins on . . .
    Leonardo da Vinci,
        may your bones
           become the brush of a Cubist painter
for grabbing me by the throat—your hands dripping with paint—
and sticking in my mouth like a gold-plated tooth
this cursed smile . . .

Part Two
The Flight

Ah, friends, Gioconda is in a bad way . . .
Take it from me,
      if she didn't have hopes
          of getting word from afar,
she'd steal a guard's pistol,
        and aiming to give the color of death
to her lips' cursed smile,
        she'd empty it into her canvas breast . . .

FROM GIOCONDA'S DIARY

O that Leonardo da Vinci's brush
had conceived me
          under the gilded sun of China!
That the painted mountain behind me
had been a sugar-loaf Chinese mountain,
that the pink-white color of my long face
           could fade,
that my eyes were almond-shaped!
And if only my smile
        could show what I feel in my heart!
Then in the arms of him who is far away
        I could have roamed through China . . .

FROM THE AUTHOR'S NOTEBOOK

I had a heart-to-heart talk with Gioconda today.
The hours flew by
        one after another

like the pages of a spell-binding book.
And the decision we reached
will cut like a knife
                    Gioconda's life
                              in two.
Tomorrow night you'll see us carry it out . . .

The clock of Notre Dame
                    strikes midnight.
Midnight
          midnight.
Who knows at this very moment
          which drunk is killing his wife?
Who knows at this very moment
          which ghost
                    is haunting the halls
                              of a castle?
Who knows at this very moment
          which thief
                    is surmounting
                              the most unsurmountable wall?
Midnight . . . Midnight . . .
Who knows at this very moment . . .
I know very well that in every novel
                    this is the darkest hour.
Midnight
          strikes fear into the heart of every reader . . .
But what could I do?
When my monoplane landed
                    on the roof of the Louvre,
the clock of Notre Dame
                    struck midnight.
And, strangely enough, I wasn't afraid

as I patted the aluminum rump of my plane
                        and stepped down on the roof...
Uncoiling the fifty-fathom-long rope wound around my waist,
I lowered it outside Gioconda's window
like a vertical bridge between heaven and hell.
I blew my shrill whistle three times.
And I got an immediate response
to those three shrill whistles.
Gioconda threw open her window.
This poor farmer's daughter
                        done up as the Virgin Mary
chucked her gilded frame
and, grabbing hold of the rope, pulled herself up...

SI-YA-U, my friend,
                you were truly lucky to fall
to a lion-hearted woman like her...

FROM GIOCONDA'S DIARY

This thing called an airplane
                        is a winged iron horse.
Below us is Paris
        with its Eiffel Tower—
                a sharp-nosed, pock-marked, moon-like face.
We're climbing,
                climbing higher.
Like an arrow of fire
                we pierce
                        the darkness.
The heavens rise overhead,
                        looming closer;
the sky is like a meadow full of flowers.
                        We're climbing,
                                climbing higher.

. . . .
. . . .
. . . .

I must have dozed off—
        I opened my eyes.
Dawn's moment of glory.
The sky a calm ocean,
our plane a ship.
I call this smooth sailing, smooth as butter.
Behind us a wake of smoke floats.
Our eyes survey blue vacancies
        full of glittering discs. . .
Below us the earth looks
        like a Jaffa orange
            turning gold in the sun. . .
By what magic have I
        climbed off the ground
            hundreds of minarets high,
and yet to gaze down at the earth
        my mouth still waters. . .

FROM THE AUTHOR'S NOTEBOOK

Now our plane swims
        within the hot winds
            swarming over Africa.
Seen from above,
        Africa looks like a huge violin.
I swear
they're playing Tchaikovsky on a cello
        on the angry dark island
            of Africa.
And waving his long hairy arms,
        a gorilla is sobbing. . .

We're crossing the Indian Ocean.
We're drinking in the air
        like a heavy, faint-smelling syrup.
And keeping our eyes on the yellow beacon of Singapore
—leaving Australia on the right,
        Madagascar on the left—
and putting our faith in the fuel in the tank,
        we're heading for the China Sea. . .

From the journal of a deckhand named John aboard a
British vessel in the China Sea

One night
    a typhoon blows up out of the blue.
Man,
    what a hurricane!
Mounted on the back of a yellow devil, the Mother of God
       whirls around and around, churning up the air.
And as luck would have it,
       I've got the watch on the foretop.
The huge ship under me
    looks about this big!
The wind is roaring
    blast
        after blast,
           blast
             after blast. . .
The mast quivers like a strung bow.(*)

(*)What business do you have being way up there?
    Christ, man, what do you think you are—a stork?
                N.H.

Oops, now we're shooting sky-high—
                    my head splits the clouds.
Oops, now we're sinking to the bottom—
                    my fingers comb the ocean floor.
We're leaning to the left, we're leaning to the right—
that is, we're leaning larboard and starboard.
My God, we just sank!
                    Oh no! This time we're sure to go under!
The waves
leap over my head
                    like Bengal tigers.
Fear
    leads me on
                    like a coffee-colored Javanese whore.
This is no joke—this is the China Sea...(*)

Okay, let's keep it short.
PLOP...
What's that?
A rectangular piece of canvas dropped from the air
                                    into the crow's nest.
The canvas
            was some kind of woman!
It struck me this madame who came from the sky
                    would never understand
                    our seamen's talk and ways.
I got right down and kissed her hand,
        and making like a poet, I cried:
"O you canvas woman who fell from the sky!
Tell me, which goddess should I compare you to?
Why did you descend here? What is your large purpose?"

(*)The deckhand has every right to be afraid.
    The rage of the China Sea is not to be taken lightly.
                                    N.H.

She replied:
"I fell
        from a 550-horsepower plane.
My name is Gioconda,
        I come from Florence.
I must get to Shanghai
                as soon as possible."

FROM GIOCONDA'S DIARY

    The wind died down,
            the sea calmed down.
The ship makes strides toward Shanghai.
The sailors dream,
            rocking in their sailcloth hammocks.
A song of the Indian Ocean plays
                on their thick fleshy lips:
"The fire of the Indochina sun
warms the blood
            like Malacca wine.
They lure sailors to gilded stars,
                those Indochina nights,
                    those Indochina nights.

Slant-eyed yellow Bornese cabin boys
knifed in Singapore bars
paint the iron-belted barrels blood-red.
Those Indochina nights, those Indochina nights.

A ship plunges on
to Canton,
55,000 tons.
Those Indochina nights...

As the moon swims in the heavens
      like the corpse of a blue-eyed sailor
           tossed overboard,
Bombay watches, leaning on its elbow. . .
                   Bombay moon,
                       Arabian Sea.
The fire of the Indochina sun
warms the blood
      like Malacca wine.
They lure sailors to gilded stars,
               those Indochina nights,
                  those Indochina nights. . ."

Part Three
Gioconda's End

Shanghai is a big port,
an excellent port.
Its ships are taller than
horned mandarin mansions.
My, my!
What a strange place, this Shanghai...

In the blue river boats
with straw sails float.
In the straw-sailed boats
naked coolies sort rice,
                    raving of rice...
My, my!
What a strange place, this Shanghai...

Shanghai is a big port.
The whites' ships are tall,
the yellows' boats small.
Shanghai is pregnant with a red-headed child.
My, my!

FROM THE AUTHOR'S NOTEBOOK

Last night
when the ship entered the harbor
Gioconda's foot kissed the land.
Shanghai the soup, she the ladle,
she searched high and low for her SI-YA-U.

"Chinese work! Japanese work!
Only two people make this—
a man and a woman.

Chinese work! Japanese work!
Just look at the art
in this latest work of LI-LI-FU."

Screaming at the top of his voice,
the Chinese magician
                    LI.
His shriveled yellow spider of a hand
tossed long thin knives into the air:
one
        one more
                    one
                        one more
                                five
                                    one more.
Tracing lightning-like circles in the air,
six knives flew up in a steady stream.
Gioconda looked,
            she kept looking,
                    she'd still be looking
but, like a large-colored Chinese lantern,
                the crowd swayed and became confused:
"Stand back! Gang way!
Chiang Kai-shek's executioner
                is hunting down a new head.
Stand back! Gang way!"

One in front and one close behind,
two Chinese shot around the corner.

The one in front ran toward Gioconda.
The one racing toward her, it was him, it was him—yes, him!
Her SI-YA-U,
                her dove.
                    SI-YA-U...
A dull hollow stadium sound surrounded them.
And in the cruel English language
                stained red with the blood
                        of yellow Asia
                            the crowd yelled:
"He's catching up,
he's catching up,
                he caught—
                        catch him!"

Just three steps away from Gioconda's arms
Chiang Kai-shek's executioner caught up.
His sword
                flashed...
Thud of cut flesh and bone.
Like a yellow sun drenched in blood
SI-YA-U's head
                rolled at her feet...
And thus on a death day
Gioconda of Florence lost in Shanghai
her smile more famous than Florence.

FROM THE AUTHOR'S NOTEBOOK

A Chinese bamboo frame.
In the frame is a painting.
Under the painting, a name:
                    "La Gioconda"...
In the frame is a painting:
                the eyes of the painting are burning, burning.

In the frame is a painting:
    the painting in the frame comes alive, alive.
And suddenly
    the painting jumped out of the frame
        as if from a window;
            her feet hit the ground.
And just as I shouted her name
she stood up straight before me:
    the giant woman of a colossal struggle.

She walked ahead,
    I trailed behind.
From the blazing red Tibetan sun
to the China Sea
        we went and came,
        we came and went.
I saw
    Gioconda
        sneak out under the cover of darkness
through the gates of a city in enemy hands;
I saw her
in a skirmish of drawn bayonets
        strangle a British officer;
I saw her
at the head of a blue stream swimming with stars
wash the lice from her dirty shirt. . .

Huffing and puffing, a wood-burning engine
dragged behind it
forty red cars seating forty people each.
The cars passed one by one.
In the last car I saw her
standing watch:
        a frayed lambskin hat on her head,
            boots on her feet,
        a leather jacket on her back. . .

Ah, my patient reader!
Now we find ourselves in the French
military court in Shanghai.
The bench:
four generals, fourteen colonels,
and an armed black Congolese regiment.
The accused:
Gioconda.
The attorney for the defense:
an overly crazed
—that is, overly artistic—
                    French painter.
The scene is set.
                    We're starting.

The defense attorney presents his case:

"Gentlemen,
this masterpiece
        that stands in your presence as the accused
is the most accomplished daughter of a great artist.
Gentlemen,
        this masterpiece. . .
Gentlemen. . .
My mind is on fire. . .
Gentlemen. . .
        Renaissance. . .
Gentlemen,
        this masterpiece—
                twice this masterpiece. . .
Gentlemen, uniformed gentlemen. . ."

"C-U-U-U-T!
          Enough.
Stop sputtering like a jammed machine gun!
Bailiff,
          read the verdict."

The bailiff reads the verdict:

"The laws of France
          have been violated in China
by the above-named Gioconda, daughter of one Leonardo.
Accordingly,
          we sentence the accused
                    to death
                              by burning.
And tomorrow night at moonrise,
a Senegalese regiment
                    will execute said decision
                              of this military court. . ."

THE BURNING

Shanghai is a big port.
The whites' ships are tall,
the yellows' boats small.
A thick whistle.
                    A thin Chinese scream.
A ship steaming into the harbor
                    capsized a straw-sailed boat. . .
Moonlight.
Night.
Handcuffed,
          Gioconda waits.
Blow, wind, blow. . .

A voice:
"All right, the lighter.
Burn, Gioconda, burn..."
A silhouette advances,
a flash...
They lit the lighter
and set Gioconda on fire.
The flames painted Gioconda red.
She laughed with a smile that came from her heart.
Gioconda burned laughing...

Art, Shmart, Masterpiece, Shmasterpiece, And So On,
   And So Forth,
      Immortality, Eternity—
                  H-E-E-E-E-E-E-E-E-E-E-Y...

   "HERE ENDS MY TALE'S CONTENDING,
   THE REST IS LIES UNENDING..."
                    THE END

1929

A SPRING PIECE LEFT IN THE MIDDLE

Taut, thick fingers punch
the teeth of my typewriter.
Three words are down on paper
                    in capitals:
SPRING
        SPRING
                SPRING...
And me—poet, proofreader,
the man who's forced to read
two thousand bad lines
        every day
                for two liras—
why,
        since spring
                has come, am I
                        still sitting here
                        like a ragged
                                black chair?
My head puts on its cap by itself,
        I fly out of the printer's,
                I'm on the street.
The lead dirt of the composing room
                        on my face,
seventy-five cents in my pocket.
                        SPRING IN THE AIR...

In the barbershops
        they're powdering
                the sallow cheeks
                        of the pariah of Publishers Row.
And in the store windows
        three-color bookcovers
                flash like sunstruck mirrors.

But me,
I don't have even a book of ABC's
that lives on this street
and carries my name on its door!
But what the hell...
I don't look back,
the lead dirt of the composing room
                    on my face,
seventy-five cents in my pocket.
            SPRING IN THE AIR...
                    *
This piece got left in the middle.
It rained and swamped the lines.
But oh! what I would have written...
The starving writer sitting on his three-thousand-page
                    three-volume manuscript
wouldn't stare at the window of the kebab joint
but with his shining eyes would take
the Armenian bookseller's dark plump daughter by storm...
The sea would start smelling sweet.
Spring would rear up
            like a sweating red mare
and, leaping onto its bare back,
                    I'd ride it
            into the water.
Then
        my typewriter would follow me
                every step of the way.
I'd say:
        "Oh, don't do it!
        Leave me alone for an hour..."
Then
my head—my hair falling out—
            would shout into the distance:
                "I AM IN LOVE..."

•

I'm twenty-seven,
she's seventeen.
"Blind Cupid,
lame Cupid,
both blind and lame Cupid
said, *Love this girl*,"
                  I was going to write;
                  I couldn't say it
                      but still can!
But if
      it rained,
if the lines I wrote got swamped,
if I have twenty-five cents left in my pocket,
                    what the hell . . .
Hey, spring is here spring is here spring
                    spring is here!
My blood is budding inside me!

20 and 21 April 1929

ON SHIRTS, PANTS, CLOTH CAPS, AND FELT HATS

If there are those
who'd call
      me
         "an enemy
            of a clean shirt,"
they should see a picture of my great teacher.
The master of masters, Marx, pawned
            his jacket,
and he ate maybe one meal every four days;
yet
   his awesome beard
   cascaded
      down a spotless
         snow-white
   starched shirt . . .
And since when did pressed pants get the death sentence?
Wise guys
      should read our history here, too:
"In 1848, as bullets parted his hair,
   he'd wear
         pants of genuine English wool
           in true English style,
         creased and waxed
           à l'anglaise—
       the greatest of men, Engels . . .
When Vladimir Ilyich Ulyanov Lenin stood
like a fire-breathing giant on the barricades,
he wore a collar
         and a tie as well . . . "
As for me
who's just another proletarian poet
—Marxist-Leninist consciousness,
         thirty kilos of bones,
           seven liters of blood,

a couple kilometers
                    of blood vessels,
          muscles, flesh, skin, and nerves—
the cloth cap on my head
          doesn't tell
                    what's in it
any more than my only felt hat
          makes me a tool
                    of the past that's passing . . .
But
     if I wear a cloth cap
six days a week,
it's so that once a week
          when I'm out with my girl
                    I can wear
                              clean
                                        my only felt hat . . .
Except
why don't I have *two* felt hats?
What do you say, master?
Am I lazy?
No!
To bind pages
          twelve hours a day,
          to stand on my feet
                    till I drop,
          is hard work . . .
Am I totally stupid?
No!
For instance,
          I could hardly be
                    as backward
          as Mr. So-and-So . . .
Am I a fool?
Well,
     not

completely...
Maybe a bit careless...
But all the time
      the real reason is that
          I'm a proletarian,
            brother,
               a proletarian!
And I'll own two felt hats
        —two *million*—
only when,
like every
      proletarian,
I own—*we* own—
      the textile mills
      of Barcelona-Habik-Mosan-Manchester!
And if n-o-o-o-o-t,
NOT!

5 February 1931

LETTER TO MY WIFE

11-11-33
Bursa Prison

My one and only!
Your last letter says:
"My head is throbbing,
        my heart is stunned!"
You say:
"If they hang you,
      if I lose you,
           I'll die!"
You'll live, my dear—
my memory will vanish like black smoke in the wind.
Of course you'll live, red-haired lady of my heart:
in the twentieth century
            grief lasts
                at most a year.

Death—
a body swinging from a rope.
My heart
        can't accept such a death.
But
you can bet
    if some poor gypsy's hairy black
          spidery hand
            slips a noose
               around my neck,
they'll look in vain for fear
          in Nazim's
            blue eyes!
In the twilight of my last morning
I
will see my friends and you,

and I'll go
to my grave
            regretting nothing but an unfinished song...

My wife!
Good-hearted,
golden,
eyes sweeter than honey—my bee!
Why did I write you
                    they want to hang me?
The trial has hardly begun,
and they don't just pluck a man's head
                            like a turnip.
Look, forget all this.
If you have any money,
                buy me some flannel underwear:
my sciatica is acting up again.
And don't forget,
a prisoner's wife
                must always think good thoughts.

THE EPIC OF SHEIK BEDREDDIN

I was reading "The Simavné Governor's Son Bedreddin," a treatise written by Mehmet Sherefeddin Effendi, Professor of Scripture at the University's School of Theology, and printed in 1925 by the Evkafi Islamiyé. I'd reached page sixty-five of the treatise. On this scripture professor's sixty-fifth page, Ducasse—who served as a private secretary to the Genoese—was saying, "At this time, a common Turkish peasant appeared in the mountainous region at the entrance to the Bay of Ionia, known by the people there as Stylarium-Karaburun. Stylarium is located across from the island of Chios. The said peasant, in preaching and giving counsel to the Turks, advised that—except for women—everything like food, clothing, livestock, and land should be considered the joint property of all the people."

The private secretary to the Genoese, who explained so simply and so clearly the counsel and advice of the common Turkish peasant in Stylarium, passed before me with his black velvet robe, pointed beard, and long, sallow, ceremonious face. That Mustafa, the greatest disciple of the Simavné governor's son Bedreddin, should be called "common" made me smile—at both senses of the word. Then I suddenly thought of the author of the treatise, Mehmet Sherefeddin Effendi, who wrote, "That Mustafa, who advised making such things as foodstuffs, livestock, and land joint public property, should exempt women seems to be an evasion and a deception he chose to practice in the face of public opinion. For certainly his sheik, who believed in the oneness of creation, never authorized Mustafa to make this exception."

This scripture professor was, I found, so well-versed in geomancy that he could divine in the earth thrown over the centuries the innermost thoughts of people. And I remembered two sentences from Marx and Engels: "The bourgeois sees in his wife a mere means of production. When he hears the means of production are to be socialized, naturally he can only conclude this socialization will extend to women as well."

Why shouldn't the professor at the University's theological school think about Bedreddin's medieval peasant socialism what the bourgeois thinks about modern industrial socialism? From the point of view of theology, aren't women property?

I closed the book. My eyes burned, but I wasn't sleepy. I looked at the Chemin de Fer watch hanging on a nail over my bed. It was almost two. I lit a cigarette. Then another. I listened to the sounds circulating in the hot, still air of the prison ward, heavy-smelling like stagnant water. The ward, with its sweating cement and twenty-eight men besides me, was asleep. The guards in the towers blew their whistles again—they were more frequent and more piercing that night. Whenever the whistles went wild with a mad contagion like that—possibly for no reason at all—I felt I was on a ship sinking in the dark night.

From the ward above came the rattle of the chained bandits on death row. Their case was before the appeals court. Ever since the rainy night they returned with their sentences, they'd paced that way, clanking their chains till morning.

When we were taken out to the back yard during the day, how many times I stared up at their windows! Three men. Two sat in the window on the right, one in the window on the left. They said the one sitting by himself got caught first and turned in his friends. He also smoked the most cigarettes.

All three wrapped their arms around the iron bars. Though they could see the sea and mountains very well from up there, they only looked down at us in the yard—at people.

I never heard their voices. In the whole prison they were the only ones who never sang—not even once. And if their chains, which spoke like that only at night, suddenly fell silent early one morning, the prison would know three long white shirts hung in the most crowded square of the city, chests numbered.

I needed an aspirin. My palms burned. My head was full of Bedreddin and Mustafa. If I could have pushed myself a little more, if my head hadn't ached so much that my eyes blurred, I'd have seen—among the clattering swords, neighing horses, cracking whips, and weeping women and children of the distant past—the faces of Bedreddin and Mustafa like two bright words of hope.

My eyes fell on the book I'd just put down on the cement. The cover, half faded from the sun, was the purple of sour cherries, and the title was written in Arabic script like a sultan's monogram. The torn edges of the yellowed pages stuck out under the cover. I thought: Bedreddin must be rescued from this theology professor's Arabic script, antique pen-case, reed pen, and blotting powder. In my head were lines from Arabshah, Ashikpashazadé, Neshri, Idris of Bitlis, Ducasse, and even Sherefeddin Effendi—lines I'd read until I knew them by heart:

There is a strong possibility that the date of Bedreddin's birth would have to be placed around 1359.

Bedreddin, who completed his education in Egypt, remained there many years and doubtless attained great learning in that milieu.

Upon his return to Edirné from Egypt, he found his parents still living.

While his arrival there could have been for the purpose of visiting his mother and father, the possibility also exists that he had been invited by Prince Musa, who had jurisdiction over the city.

When Sultan Mehmet I came to power by defeating his brothers, he banished Sheik Bedreddin to Iznik.

In the preface to Foundations, *which he completed there, the Sheik wrote, "The fire in my heart has burst into flame. And it's mounting daily, so that were my heart wrought iron, it would melt."*

When they exiled the Sheik to Iznik, his chief disciple, Mustafa, removed to Aydin. He made his way from there to Karaburun.

•

He went around saying, "Just as I could have the use of your posses-sions, in the same way you could have the use of mine." After he had won over the common peasants with such preachings, he tried to convert the Christians. Although Sultan Mehmet's Saruhan governor Sisman moved against this false prophet, his forces could not penetrate the narrow passes of Stylarium.

When the Simavné governor's son Bedreddin heard how Mustafa's situation was improving, he fled Iznik. Reaching Sinope, he eventually boarded ship and landed in the province of Walachia. From there he fled to the Mad Forest in Dobruja.

Meanwhile, word of the intrigues and heresies of the agitator Mustafa, the aforesaid Bedreddin's appointed representative in the province of Aydin, reached Sultan Mehmet's ear. Immediately an imperial edict was handed down to Prince Murad, ruler of Amasya and Little Rumelia, that he set about eliminating the heretic Mustafa by assem-bling a regiment of Anatolian soldiers and descending on him in the province of Aydin with a full complement of men and equipment.

Mustafa, with a force of nearly ten thousand of his seditious and subversive followers, stood up to defy the Prince.

A great battle ensued.

After much blood was spilled, the godless forces were vanquished with divine guidance.

The survivors were taken to Seljuk. Even the most terrible tortures applied to Mustafa could not turn him from his obsession. Mustafa was stretched on a cross on a camel. After his hands were nailed to the wood, he was led through the city in a great procession. His conspirators who remained loyal to him were executed before his eyes. With the words "Long live Grand Sultan Mustafa!" they relinquished their souls and died at peace.

Lastly, they tore Mustafa limb from limb and inspected the ten provinces; satisfied, they granted the soldiers fiefdoms. Bayezid Pasha returned to Manisa, and there he found Bedreddin's disciple Kemal. And there he hanged him.

Meanwhile, Bedreddin's position in Dobruja had improved. People came from everywhere and gathered around him. He was on the verge of uniting all the people. For this reason, Sultan Mehmet's personal intervention became necessary.

On the advice of Bayezid Pasha, certain persons infiltrated Bedreddin's professional followers and disciples. And taking all the necessary precautions, they arrested Bedreddin in the forest and tied him up.

They brought him before Sultan Mehmet in Serrai. Accompanying Sultan Mehmet was an advisor named Mevlana Haydar, who had recently arrived from Persia. Mevlana Haydar declared: "Under Islamic law, this man's death is holy, his substance unholy."

From there they carried the Simavné governor's son Bedreddin to the market place and hanged him outside a shop. After a few days, some of his unclean disciples appeared and took him away. He has disciples in that region to this day.

My head was splitting. I checked my watch. It had stopped. The rattle of chains upstairs let up. Only one of them still paced, probably the one who sat alone in the window on the left.

I wished I could hear an Anatolian song. It seemed to me that if the highwaymen started singing that mountain song again, my headache would disappear on the spot.

I lit another cigarette. I reached down and picked up Mehmet Sherefeddin Effendi's treatise from the cement. A wind had come up outside. It grumbled under the window, shutting out the sounds of the sea, chains, and whistles. It must have been rocky below the window. How many times we'd tried to look down there where our wall met the sea! But it was no use: the window's iron bars were too close together for us to stick our heads out. So there we saw the sea only on the horizon.

The lathe-operator Shefik's bed was next to mine. He rolled over in his sleep, mumbling something. The wedding quilt his wife had sent him slipped off. I covered him up.

I turned back to page sixty-five of the scripture professor at the theological school. I'd read only a couple lines from the First Secretary to the Genoese, when I heard a voice through the pain in my head.

The voice said: "Silently I crossed the waves of the sea to be here with you."

I spun around. There was someone at the window. That's who was talking.

"Have you forgotten what Ducasse, First Secretary to the Genoese, wrote? Don't you remember he spoke of a Cretan monk who lived on Chios in a monastery called Turlut? Me, 'one of Mustafa's dervishes,' didn't I used to visit that monk across the waves of the sea this way, bareheaded, barefoot, wrapped in a piece of cloth?"

I looked at who spoke these words standing as big as life outside the bars, where there was nothing to hold on to. He really was dressed as he said. His seamless robe flowed down all white.

Now, writing these lines years later, I think of the theology professor. I don't know if Sherefeddin Effendi is dead or alive. But if he's alive and reads what I write, he'll say, "What a fake! He claims to be a materialist and then, like the Cretan monk, goes on—centuries after the event!—about talking with Mustafa's disciple who silently crosses seas."

And I can almost hear the divine laughter with which the master of scripture will follow these words.

But no matter. Let his excellency laugh. And I'll tell my story.

Suddenly my headache was gone. I got out of bed and went up to him in the window. He took my hand. We left the sleeping ward with its sweating cement and twenty-eight men besides me.

Suddenly I found myself where we could never see—on the rocks where our wall met the sea. Side by side, Mustafa's disciple and I crossed the waves of the dark sea and went back through the years—centuries back—to the time of Sultan Mehmet I.

This journey is the adventure I want to recount. And the spectacle of sounds, colors, shapes, and events I witnessed on this trip I'll try to capture piece by piece and mostly—according to an old habit—in assorted long and short lines with an occasional rhyme. Like this:

1

On the divan, Bursa silk in green-branching red boughs;
a blue garden of Kutahya tiles on the wall;
wine in silver pitchers;
and lambs in copper pots roasted golden brown.
Strangling his own brother with a bowstring
—anointing himself with a gold bowl of his brother's blood—
Sultan Mehmet had ascended the throne and was sovereign.
Mehmet was sovereign,
but in the land of Osman
the wind was a fruitless cry, a death song.
The peasants' work done by the light of their eyes
and the sweat of their brows
                              was a fief.
The cracked water jugs were dry—
at the springs, horsemen stood twirling their mustaches.
On the roads, a traveler could hear the wail of men without land
                              and land without men.
And as foaming horses neighed and swords clashed
            outside the castle door where all roads led,
the market place was in chaos,
            the guilds had lost faith in their masters.
In short, there was a sovereign, a fief, a wind, a wail.
                    •

2
This is Iznik Lake.
Still.
Dark.
Deep.
It's like a well
    in the mountains.

Around here lakes
are smoky.
Their fish taste flat,
their marshes breed malaria,
and the men die before their beards turn white.

This is Iznik Lake.
Beside it stands the town of Iznik.
In the town of Iznik
the blacksmith's anvil is a broken heart.
The children go hungry.
The women's breasts are like dried fish.
And the young men don't sing.

This is the town of Iznik.
This is a house
in the workers' quarter.
In this house
lives an old man named Bedreddin.
Small build,
        big beard—
                    white.
Eyes like a child's, sly and slanted,
and yellow fingers like reeds.

Bedreddin
sits

on a white sheepskin.
He's writing *Foundations*
                in Persian script.
Down on their knees, they sit across from him.
And from a distance
they look at him as if staring at a mountain.
Head shaved,
eyebrows bushy,
he looks:
tall and rangy Mustafa.
He looks:
hawk-nosed Kemal.
They don't tire of looking
and cannot look enough—
they gaze at the Iznik exile Bedreddin.

3
A barefoot woman is crying on the shore.
And in the lake
                an empty fishing boat has broken loose,
                floating on the water
                like a dead bird.
It goes where the water takes it
across the lake to be smashed on the mountains.

Evening comes to Iznik Lake.
Thick-voiced horsemen in the mountains
slit the sun's throat
                and drain the blood into the lake.
On the shore a barefoot woman is crying,
the wife of the fisherman chained in the castle
                                for taking a carp.

                        •

Evening comes to Iznik Lake.
Bedreddin kneels,
           cups water in his hands, and stands up.
And as the water
slips through his fingers
and returns to the lake,
                    he says to himself:
"The fire in my heart
has burst into flame
and is mounting daily.
Were my heart wrought iron, it could not resist,
it would melt...
I will come out now and declare myself!
Men of the land, we will conquer the land.
And proving the power of knowledge
        and the mystery of Oneness,
we'll abolish the laws of nations and religions..."(*)
                    *
The next day,
as the boat was smashed in the lake,
           a head was cut off in the castle,
                    and a woman cried on the shore,
           and as the one from Simavné
           wrote his *Foundations,*
           Kemal and Mustafa
           kissed
                    their sheik's hand.
           Saddling their roan horses,
           they rode out through the Iznik gates,

(*)"I will come out now and declare myself, so that my believers and I may
come into possession of the world. And with the power of knowledge and the
revelation of the mystery of Oneness, we will abolish the pretenders' laws and
religions" (the Sheik's words as reported by the author of *Eight Heavens* in M.S.'s
translation).

each with a naked sword at his side
and a handwritten book in his saddlebag.
The book:
> Bedreddin's *Illuminations*.

4

After Mustafa and Kemal took their leave of Bedreddin and
mounted their horses and rode off, one for Aydin and the other
for Manisa, I left with my guide for Konya, and one day, upon
reaching the Haymana plain,

we heard Mustafa had appeared
in Karaburun in Aydin.
He preached Bedreddin's word
to an audience of peasants.

We heard: "That the people might be freed of their suffering
and the earth's flesh be made pure
              as a fifteen-year-old boy's,
the landowners have been slaughtered wholesale
and the lords' fiefdoms made public land."

We heard . . .
Can you hear such things and sit still?
Early one morning,
as a lone bird sang on the Haymana plain,
we ate olives under a scrawny willow.
"Let's go,"
              we said,
"and see.
Grab
      a plow,
and let's us work this brother's land
                              for a stretch,"
                              we said.

We hit mountains
and left them behind...

Friends,
I didn't travel alone.
One afternoon I told my companion:
                              "We're here."
                              I said: "Look.
The earth that was weeping back there
is laughing like a child before our eyes.
Look, the figs are like huge emeralds,
and the vines can barely hold the amber clusters.
Look at the fish jumping in the reed baskets—
their sparkling wet skin shimmers,
and their meat is white and tender
                    like a young lamb's."
I said: "Look,
here people are fruitful like the earth, sun, and sea;
here the sea, sun, and earth bear fruit like people."

5

When we left the sovereign lords' fiefdoms behind and entered
Mustafa's country, we were met by three young men. All three
wore seamless white robes like my guide's. The first had a curly
ebony beard, passionate eyes the same color, and a big hooked
nose. He used to be of Moses's faith; now he was one of Mustafa's
braves.

The second had a round chin and a straight nose. A Greek
sailor from Chios, he, too, was Mustafa's disciple.

The third was of medium height and broad-shouldered. When
I think of him now, I liken him to Hussein who sang that moun-
tain song in the highwaymen's ward. But Hussein came from
Erzurum; this one was from Aydin.

The one from Aydin spoke first: "Are you friend or foe? If

you're friends, welcome; if you're enemies, your next breath will be your last."

"We're friends," we said.

Upon which we learned that in the high passes of Karaburun they'd just wiped out the army of the Saruhan governor Sisman, who tried to return the lands to their sovereign lords.

Again the one who looked like Hussein spoke: "If, on our brothers' table stretching from here to the sea off Karaburun, the figs are so honeyed this year, the grain so heavy, and the olives so fat, it's because we watered them with the blood of the gilt-jacketed despoilers."

The joyful news was very great.

"Then let's return immediately and bear the glad tidings to Bedreddin," my guide said.

Taking along Anastos, the sailor from Chios, we left the brothers' land we'd barely set foot in, and plunged once more into the darkness of Osman's sons.

We found Bedreddin in Iznik on the lakeshore. It was morning. The air was damp and sad.

"Now it's our turn," Bedreddin said. "We'll leave for Rumelia."

We left Iznik at night, pursued by horsemen. The darkness was like a wall between them and us. And we could hear their hoofbeats behind it. My guide led the way, Bedreddin's horse between my roan horse and Anastos's. We three were like mothers, and Bedreddin was our child. We were breathless for fear they might do him harm. We were like three children, and Bedreddin was our father. Whenever the hoofbeats behind the wall of darkness seemed to come nearer, we moved closer to Bedreddin.

Hiding by day and traveling by night, we reached Sinope. There we set sail.

6
Stars and a sailboat alone

on a sea one night.

On a sea one night a sailboat
                    alone with the stars.
The stars without number.
The sails down.
The water dark
          and flat as far as the eye could see.
Blond Anastos and the islander Bekir
                    manned the oars.
I sat in the bow
          with Bull Salih.
And Bedreddin,
          fingers buried in his beard,
                    listened to the oars splash.

  "Well, Bedreddin,"
          I said.
            "We see nothing but stars
                    above the sleeping sails.
          No whispers stir the air.
          And no sounds
                    rise from the sea.
          Only mute, dark water,
          only its sleep."
The little old man with the white beard bigger than himself
                              laughed.
                    He said:
          "Never mind the stillness—
          the deep sleeps to awake."

Stars and a sailboat alone
                    on a sea one night.
One night a boat sailed the Black Sea
                    headed for the Mad Forest,
                    the Sea of Trees . . .
                         •

7

We landed in this forest, this Mad Forest,
and pitched tents in the Sea of Trees.
We flew a falcon from every branch to every village
        with the message "You know why we have come,
                        you know the trouble in our hearts."

Each falcon brought back a hundred lionhearts.
They all came—the peasant torching his master's crop,
                        the apprentice leaving his shop,
                                the serf breaking his chains.
All those like us in Rumelia came,
        an army flowing to the Sea of Trees.

What pandemonium!
A blur
        of horses, men, spears, iron, leaves,
        leather, beech branches, oak roots.
Since the Mad Forest went mad,
it hadn't seen such revelry
                or heard such a din . . .

8

Leaving Anastos in Bedreddin's camp in the Mad Forest, my
guide and I went down to Gallipoli. Someone long before us
swam this strait—for love, I guess. We, too, swam across to the
other side. But what made us quick as fish was not the desire to
see a woman's face by moonlight but the need to reach Karaburun
via Izmir with news—this time, for Mustafa from his sheik.

When we stopped at a caravanserai near Izmir, we learned
Bayezid Pasha, who led the Sultan's twelve-year-old son Murad
by the hand, was mobilizing Anatolian soldiers.

We didn't waste time in Izmir. We had just left the city by the
Aydin road, when we came upon four gentlemen resting in a

vineyard and chatting under a walnut tree while they waited for the watermelons they'd lowered into a well to cool. They all dressed differently; three wore turbans, one a fez. We exchanged greetings. One of the turbans was the historian Neshri. He said, "Sultan Mehmet has sent Bayezid Pasha against Mustafa, who has invited the people to join a religion of libertinism."

The second turban was Shekerullah bin Shehabeddin. He said, "Numerous persons have united around this mystic. And many of their practices, which are clearly contrary to Islamic law, have come to light."

The third turbaned personage was the historian Ashik-pashazadé. He said, "Question: if the aforementioned Mustafa is torn limb from limb, will he go with faith or without? Answer: God alone knows, for it is not given to us to know the final state of his soul."

The gentleman in the fez was the scripture professor at the theological school. He looked at us, blinked his eyes, and gave us a sly smile. He didn't say a word.

At that, we dug our spurs into our horses and left. Leaving in the dust of our hooves the gentlemen chatting under a walnut tree in a vineyard while cooling the watermelons they'd lowered into a well, we reached Karaburun and Mustafa.

9
It was hot.
Hot.
The heat
            was a dull knife dripping blood.
It was hot.
The clouds were full.
The clouds were about
                  to burst.
Motionless, he looked:
            like two eagles, his eyes dived

down from the rocks
into the plain.
There the softest, hardest,
most generous, thriftiest,
most
loving,
biggest, most beautiful woman
EARTH
was about
to give birth.

It was hot.
He looked out from the Karaburun mountains.
Brows knitted, he looked toward the horizon,
the end of this earth:
plucking the heads of children in the fields
like bloody poppies
and dragging their naked cries in its wake,
a five-star fire swept across the horizon.
It was
Prince Murad.
An imperial edict had been handed down to Prince Murad
to hasten to Aydin
and descend on Bedreddin's appointed representative, Mustafa.

It was hot.
Bedreddin's man, the heretic Mustafa, looked
—the peasant Mustafa looked—
without fear,
anger,
or a smile.
He looked
straight ahead.
He looked.
The softest, hardest,

most generous, thriftiest,
most
        loving,
biggest, most beautiful woman
                    EARTH
            was about
                to give birth.

He looked.
Bedreddin's braves looked out from the rocks at the horizon.
The end of this earth approached
                on the wings of a decreed bird of death.
Yet
    those who looked out from the rocks
had opened up this earth
like a brother's table spread for all—
this earth
with its grapes, figs, and pomegranates,
its sheep with fleece blonder than honey
                and milk thicker than honey
and its narrow-waisted, lion-maned horses.

It was hot.
He looked.
Bedreddin's braves looked out at the horizon . . .

It was hot.
The clouds were full.
The first drop was about to fall
like a sweet word.
All
    of a sudden,
as if streaming down from the rocks,
        raining down from the sky,
            and springing up from the ground,

Bedreddin's braves faced the Prince's army
like the last act of this earth.
With flowing white robes,
                    bare heads,
                            bare feet, and bare swords . . .

A great battle took place.

Turkish peasants from Aydin,
            Greek sailors from Chios,
                    Jewish tradesmen,
Mustafa's ten thousand heretical comrades
plunged into the forest of enemies like ten thousand axes.

The ranks of green-and-red flags,
            inlaid shields,
                    and bronze helmets
were torn apart,
but when the day descended into night in pouring rain,
the ten thousand were two thousand.

That they might sing as one voice
and together pull the nets from the water,
that they might all work iron like lace
and all together plow the earth,
that they might eat the honeyed figs together,
that they might say,
                    "Everywhere
                        all together
                            in everything
                            but the lover's cheek,"
the ten thousand lost eight thousand . . .

They were defeated.

The victors wiped their bloody swords
            on the flowing white robes
                of the defeated.
And the earth brothers had worked all together
like a song sung together
was ripped up
                by the hooves of horses bred in the Edirné palace.

Don't say
        it's the necessary result
            of historical, social, and economic conditions—
                                I know!
My head bows before the thing you mention.
But my heart
        doesn't speak that language.
It says,
"O fickle Fate,
O cruel Fate!"
And they pass one by one,
shoulders slashed by whips,
                faces bloodied—
in a flash they pass,
bare feet crushing my heart—
the defeated of Karaburun pass through Aydin . . .(*)

(*)Now, as I write these lines, I think of certain young people who pass for
"leftists" and who'll say, "Well! He separates his head and heart; he says his head
accepts the historical, social, and economic conditions, but his heart still burns.
Well, well—will you look at the Marxist!" The way I thought of the scripture pro-
fessor and heard his laugh at the very beginning of this work . . .

And if I am now making such a statement, it isn't for these young people; it's
for those who are far beyond the leftist affectations of the recent discoverers of
Marxism.

If a doctor has a tubercular child, if he knows the child will die, if he accepts it
as a physiological, biological, I-don't-know-what-logical necessity, and if the child
dies, the doctor—who well knew this death was inevitable—won't he shed a
single tear?

Marx, who knew the Paris Commune would be overthrown, who knew the

•

10

They stopped at dark.
It was he who spoke:
"The city of Seljuk has set up shop.
Now whose neck, friends,
           whose neck is it now?"

The rain
       kept up.
They spoke
       and told him:
"It isn't
       set up—
               it will be.
The wind hasn't
       quit—
               it will.
His throat isn't
       slit—
               it will be."

As rain seeped into the folds of the darkness,
I appeared at their side
and said:
"Where are Seljuk's city gates?
       Show me, so I can go!
Does it have a fortress?

---

historical, social, and economic conditions necessitating its overthrow, didn't he feel the Commune's great dead pass through his heart like a "song of pain"? And wasn't there at least a touch of sadness in the voices that shouted, "The Commune is dead, long live the Commune"?

Marxists are not "mechanical men" or ROBOTS; with their flesh, blood, nerves, heads, and hearts, they are historically and socially concrete people.

Tell me, and I'll raze it!
Is there a toll?
        Speak, so I don't pay it!"

Now it was he who spoke:
"Seljuk's gates are narrow.
                        You can't come and go.
It has a fortress
                not so easy to raze.
Go away, roan-horsed brave,
                        go on your way . . ."

I said: "I can come and go!"
I said: "I can raze and set fires!"
He said: "The rain has ended,
            it's getting light.
    The headsman Ali
        is calling
                    Mustafa!
Go away, roan-horsed brave,
                        go on your way . . ."

I said: "Friends,
        let me go,
        let me go!
    Friends,
        let me see him,
        let me see him!
    Don't think
    I can't take it.
    Don't think
    I can't burn
    without letting it show!

Friends,
don't say no,
don't say no uselessly!
This isn't a pear that will snap its stem,
                        this is no pear;
it won't fall from its branch even if wounded—
this heart,
this heart is no sparrow,
        no sparrow!

Friends,
I know!
Friends,
I know how and where he is!
I know
he's gone and won't come back!
I know
he's nailed
by his hands
naked on a bloody cross
        on a camel's hump.
Friends,
let me go.
Friends,
just let me go see,
see
Bedreddin's man
Mustafa,
Mustafa!"

Two thousand men to be beheaded,
Mustafa and his cross,
headsman, block, and sword—
everything was ready,
        everything set.

A gilt-embroidered red saddlecloth,
gold stirrups,
a gray horse.
On the horse sat a thick-browed child—
the ruler of Amasya, Crown Prince Murad.
And next to him,
Bayezid Pasha—I do it on his I-don't-know-whateth decoration!

The headsman struck.
Bare necks split like pomegranates.
Like apples dropping from a green branch,
             heads fell one after another.
And as each fell,
Mustafa took a last look
from his cross.
And each head that fell
didn't turn a hair
but just said,
        "Long live
                Grand Sultan Mustafa!"
and not a word more...

11

Bayezid Pasha had gone to Manisa and found there Bedreddin's disciple Kemal, and there he hanged him. The ten provinces were inspected and returned again as fiefs to the sovereign's servant lords.

My guide and I passed through these ten provinces. Vultures circled overhead, and from time to time they swooped down in dark streams, shrieking wildly as they descended on the fresh, bloody corpses of women and children. Although the bodies of men young and old lined the roads in the sun, the fact that the birds preferred the flesh of women and children showed how glutted they were.

On the roads, we met the sovereign lords' parading troops.

As the sovereign's servant lords passed with loud-colored banners, drums, and fanfare through the sluggish wind as heavy as the air of a rotting vineyard and returned over the chopped-up earth to settle back down on their fiefs, we left the ten provinces. Gallipoli appeared in the distance, and I told my guide, "I'm beat. I can't swim across."

We found a boat.

The sea was rough. I looked at the boatman. He resembled the picture I'd torn out of a German book and hung on my wall. His thick mustache was jet-black, his beard broad and white. In all my life I'd never seen such a wide, eloquent forehead.

We were in the middle of the strait, the sea flowed nonstop, and the water foamed and slipped under our boat in the lead-painted air, when our boatman who resembled the picture in my cell said, "Freeman and slave, patrician and plebian, lord and serf, guildmaster and journeyman—in a word, the oppressor and the oppressed—stood in constant opposition to each other and carried on, now covertly, now openly, a constant struggle."

12

Upon setting foot in Rumelia, we learned Sultan Mehmet had lifted the siege of Salonika and come to Serrai. We traveled day and night to reach the Mad Forest as soon as possible.

One night, when we were resting on the roadside, three horsemen heading away from the Mad Forest rode by at full gallop toward Serrai. In one of the horsemen's saddles I made out a dark shape tied up in a sack that looked like a person. My hairs rose. I said to my guide:

I know those hoofbeats.
Those jet-black horses foaming blood
have carried prisoners tied to their saddles
at full gallop down dark roads.

I know those hoofbeats.
One morning
        they came up
to our tents like a song of friendship.
We broke bread with them.
The air was so beautiful
and the heart so hopeful,
the eye became a child again,
and our wise friend, SUSPICION, slept...

I know those hoofbeats.
One night
        they rode away
from our tents at full speed.
They knifed the sentry in the back,
and in one of their saddles,
        arms tied behind him,
                sat our most precious.

I know those hoofbeats,
and the Mad Forest knows them, too...

Before long we learned the Mad Forest did, in fact, know those hoofbeats. As soon as we stepped into our forest, we heard Bayezid Pasha had, with all the necessary precautions, planted men in the forest who infiltrated the camp, joined Bedreddin's followers, and one night, coming upon Bedreddin asleep in his tent, kidnapped him. So the three horsemen we'd met on the road were the forefathers of all the undercover agents in Ottoman history, and the prisoner they carried in their saddle was Bedreddin.

13
Rumelia, Serrai,
and an old expression:
      HIS IMPERIAL PRESENCE.

At the center,
straight as a sword stuck in the ground,
                the old man.
Facing him, the Sultan.
They looked at each other.

It was the Sultan's wish
that, before finishing off this incarnation of blasphemy,
before giving the word to the hangman,
the court should exercise its skills
and dispose of the matter properly.

A member of the court,
Mevlana Haydar by name,
a man of great learning
          who had recently arrived from Persia,
bowed his hennaed beard to divine inspiration
and, with the words "This man's substance is unholy,
              but not his blood,"
              wrapped the matter up.

They turned to Bedreddin.
They said, "You talk now."
They said, "Explain your heresy."

Bedreddin
looked out through the archway:
sunlight,
the branches of a tree turning green in the yard,
and a brook carving stones.

Bedreddin smiled.
His eyes lit up,
        and he spoke:
"Since we lost this time,
words avail not.
Don't draw it out.
Since the sentence is mine,
give it—so I can seal it . . ."

14
The rain hisses,
like words of betrayal
whispered
in fear.

The rain hisses,
like the bare white feet
of renegades
running on wet black earth.

The rain hisses.
In Serrai's market place,
across from the coppersmith's,
Bedreddin hangs from a tree.

The rain hisses.
Swinging from a bare branch,
getting wet in the rain
late on a starless night,
              the naked body of my sheik.

The rain hisses.
The market place is mute,
        Serrai is blind.

Doomed to the grief of not seeing or speaking,
Serrai's market place buries its face in its hands.

The rain hisses.

The Lathe-Operator Shefik's Shirt

The rain hissed outside. On the horizon of sea beyond the iron bars and i.. the cloudy sky above, it was morning. I remember it very clearly even today. First I felt a hand on my shoulder. I turned around. The lathe-operator Shefik fixed his shining, coal-black eyes on my face and said, "Looks like you didn't sleep last night."

Upstairs, the bandits' chains were quiet. They must have fallen asleep when it got light. In daylight the guards' whistles lost their meaning, their colors faded, and their sharp outlines, which showed only in the dark, softened.

The ward door opened from the outside. Inside, the men woke one by one.

Shefik asked, "You look a little funny—what happened?"

I told Shefik my night's adventure. "But," I said, "I saw it with my own eyes. He came right up to the window here. He wore a seamless white robe. He took my hand. I made the whole trip at his side—I mean, with his guidance."

Shefik laughed and pointed to the window: "You didn't travel with Mustafa's disciple but with my shirt. Look—I hung it out last night. It's still at the window."

By then I was laughing, too. I took down from the bars Shefik's shirt, which had served as my guide in Sheik Bedreddin's movement. Shefik put his shirt on. Everyone in the ward heard about my "trip." Ahmet said, "Now this is something you should write about. Let's have a 'Bedreddin Epic.' And I'll tell you a story myself, which you can stick at the end of your poem."

And here at the end of my poem is the story Ahmet told.

•

Ahmet's Story

It was before the Balkan War. I was nine. My grandfather and I were the guests of a peasant in Rumelia. The peasant had blue eyes and a copper beard. We ate *tarhana* soup with lots of red pepper. It was winter, one of Rumelia's dry winters that cut like a razor-sharp knife.

I can't remember the name of the village. But the guardsman who saw us off described the people of that village as the stubbornest, hardest-to-collect-taxes-from, most pigheaded peasants in the world.

According to the guardsman, they were neither Muslims nor infidels. Maybe they were Redheads. But not quite that, either.

I still remember entering the village. The sun had just about set, and the road was frozen. The hard, frozen puddles glittered like red glass.

A dog met us at the first barbed-wire fence sinking into the darkness, a huge dog looming even larger in the half-dark. He was barking.

Our driver tightened the reins. The dog attacked the horses, jumping way up to their chests.

"What's happening?" I said, and stuck my head out to see. The driver's elbow hit me in the face as he raised his whip and cracked it across the dog's head with a snake-hiss. Just then I heard a deep voice.

"Hey! You think you're the governor and anything you hit is a peasant?"

My grandfather stepped down from the carriage and greeted the dog's deep-voiced owner. They talked. Then the dog's blue-eyed, copper-bearded owner invited us to his house.

I can still hear many conversations from my childhood. I've come to understand what most of them meant only as I've grown older, and I've been surprised by some and laughed or gotten mad at others. But no grownups' talk I heard as a child affected the rest of my life like the talk between my grandfather and the blue-eyed peasant that night.

My grandfather had a soft, gentlemanly voice; the other's voice was harsh, thick, and confident.

His thick voice said: "Hanging from a bare branch of a tree in Serrai's market place by the will of the Sultan and the order of Judge Haydar from Persia, Bedreddin's naked body slowly swung from side to side. It was night. Three men came around the corner. One led an extra gray horse. Without a saddle. They stopped under the tree Bedreddin hung from. The one on the left took off his shoes and climbed the tree; the others waited below with open arms. The man in the tree started cutting the knot in the wet, soaped rope coiled like a snake around Bedreddin's thin neck under his long white beard. Suddenly the knife slipped off the rope and pierced the body's stretched neck. No blood came. The young man cutting the rope turned white. Then he leaned over and kissed the wound. Dropping the knife, he undid the knot with his hands and, like a father placing his sleeping child in its mother's arms, entrusted Bedreddin's body to the arms of those waiting below. They put the naked body on the bare horse. The man in the tree climbed down. He was the youngest. Leading the bare horse carrying the naked body, he came to our village. He buried the body under the black tree on the hill. But later the sovereign's horsemen invaded the village. When they left, the young man dug up the body under the black tree, afraid they might come back and find it. And we never saw him again."

My grandfather asked, "Are you sure that's how it happened?"

"Sure. My mother's father told it to me, and his grandfather had told him. And he'd heard it from *his* grandfather. It's always been this way...."

There were eight or ten peasants in the room besides us. They sat at the edge of the circle of half-light the fire painted red. Now and then one or another moved, and a hand, part of a face, or a shoulder entered the circle of half-light and reddened.

I heard the copper-beard's voice: "He will come back. The one hung from a tree naked will return naked."

My grandfather laughed. "This belief of yours," he said, "is like the Christians' faith. They say the prophet Jesus will come back to earth. Even some Muslims believe Jesus will appear in Damascus one day."

He didn't answer my grandfather right away. Pushing against his knees with his thick-fingered hands, he straightened up. Now his whole body was inside the red circle. I saw his face in profile. He had a long, straight nose. He spoke as if fighting: "Jesus is to be reborn with his flesh, bones, and beard. That's a lie. Bedreddin will be reborn without his bones, beard, or mustache—in the look of an eye, the words of a tongue, the breath of a chest. This I know. We are Bedreddin's people; we don't believe in any afterlife or resurrection that we can believe a dead, scattered body will gather together and be reborn. When we say Bedreddin will come again, we mean his look, words, and breath will reappear among us."

He stopped and sat down. Whether my grandfather believed in Bedreddin's return or not, I don't know. I believed it at nine and, at thirty-something, still believe it.

HYMN TO LIFE

The hair falling on your forehead
                suddenly lifted.
Suddenly something stirred on the ground.
The trees whisper
          in the dark.
Your bare arms will be cold.

Far off
        where we can't see,
                the moon must be rising.
It hasn't reached us yet,
        slipping through the leaves
                to light up your shoulder.
But I know
      a wind comes up with the moon.
The trees whisper.
Your bare arms will be cold.

From above,
from the branches lost in the dark,
                something dropped at your feet.
You moved closer to me.
Under my hand your bare flesh is like the fuzzy skin of a peach.
Neither a song of the heart nor "common sense,"
before the trees, birds, and insects
my hand on my wife's flesh
               is thinking.
Tonight my hand
          can't read or write.
It's neither loving nor unloving . . .
It's the tongue of a leopard at a spring,
            a grape leaf,
                a wolf's paw.

To move, breathe, eat, drink.
My hand is like a seed
        splitting open underground.
Neither a song of the heart nor "common sense,"
neither loving nor unloving,
my hand on my wife's flesh
        is the hand of the first man.
Like a root that finds water underground,
it says to me:
"To eat, drink, cold, hot, struggle, smell, color—
not to live in order to die
but to die to live . . . "

And now
as red female hair blows across my face,
as something stirs on the ground,
as the trees whisper in the dark,
and as the moon rises far off
        where we can't see,
my hand on my wife's flesh
before the trees, birds, and insects,
I want the right of life,
of the leopard at the spring, of the seed splitting open—
        I want the right of the first man.

1937

LETTERS FROM A MAN IN SOLITARY

1
I carved your name on my watchband
with my fingernail.
Where I am, you know,
I don't have a pearl-handled jackknife
(they won't give me anything sharp)
                or a plane tree with its head in the clouds.
Trees may grow in the yard,
but I'm not allowed
                        to see the sky overhead. . .
How many others are in this place?
I don't know.
I'm alone far from them,
they're all together far from me.
To talk to anyone besides myself
                        is forbidden.
So I talk to myself.
But I find my conversation so boring,
                my dear wife, that I sing songs.
And what do you know,
that awful, always off-key voice of mine
                touches me so
                        that my heart breaks.
And just like the barefoot orphan
        lost in the snow
in those old sad stories, my heart
—with moist blue eyes
and a little red runny nose—
                wants to snuggle up in your arms.
It doesn't make me blush
                that right now
                        I'm this weak,
                                this selfish,
                                        this *human* simply.

No doubt my state can be explained
physiologically, psychologically, etc.
Or maybe it's
             this barred window,
                   this earthen jug,
                          these four walls,
                   which for months have kept me from hearing
                   another human voice.

It's five o'clock, my dear.
Outside,
             with its dryness,
                   eerie whispers,
                                mud roof,
and lame, skinny horse
       standing motionless in infinity
—I mean, it's enough to drive the man inside crazy with grief—
outside, with all its machinery and all its art,
a plains night comes down red on treeless space.

Again today, night will fall in no time.
A light will circle the lame, skinny horse.
And the treeless space, in this hopeless landscape
stretched out before me like the body of a hard man,
will suddenly be filled with stars.
We'll reach the inevitable end once more,
which is to say the stage is set
again today for an elaborate nostalgia.
Me,
the man inside,
once more I'll exhibit my customary talent,
and singing an old-fashioned lament
in the reedy voice of my childhood,
once more, by God, it will crush my unhappy heart
to hear you inside my head,

so far
away, as if I were watching you
in a smoky, broken mirror...

2
It's spring outside, my dear wife, spring.
Outside on the plain, suddenly the smell
of fresh earth, birds singing, etc.
It's spring, my dear wife,
the plain outside sparkles...
And inside the bed comes alive with bugs,
the water jug no longer freezes,
and in the morning sun floods the concrete...
The sun—
every day till noon now
it comes and goes
from me, flashing off
and on...
And as the day turns to afternoon, shadows climb the walls,
the glass of the barred window catches fire,
and it's night outside,
a cloudless spring night...
And inside this is spring's darkest hour.
In short, the demon called freedom,
with its glittering scales and fiery eyes,
possesses the man inside
especially in spring...
I know this from experience, my dear wife,
from experience...

3
Sunday today.
Today they took me out in the sun for the first time.
And I just stood there, struck for the first time in my life
                         by how far away the sky is,
                         how blue
                         and how wide.
Then I respectfully sat down on the earth.
I leaned back against the wall.
For a moment no trap to fall into,
no struggle, no freedom, no wife.
Only earth, sun, and me. . .
I am happy.

1938

ON DEATH AGAIN

My wife,
        life of my life,
                my Pirayé,
I'm thinking about death,
which means my arteries
                are hardening...
One day
        when it's snowing,
or one night
or
    in the heat of one noon,
which of us will die first,
how
        and where?
How
        and what will be
the last sound the one dying hears,
                the last color seen,
the first movement of the one left behind,
                the first words,
                        the first food tasted?
Maybe we will die far apart.
The news
        will come screaming,
or someone will just hint at it
and go away, leaving alone
                the one left behind...
And the one left behind
        will be lost in the crowd.
I mean, that's life...
And all these possibilities,
                what year in the 1900's,
                which month,

which day,
what hour?

My wife,
          life of my life,
                    my Piraye,
I'm thinking about death,
about our life passing.
I'm sad,
          at peace,
                    and proud.
Whoever dies first,
however
and wherever we die,
you and I
          can say we loved
each other
and the people's greatest cause
                    —we fought for it—
we can say
          "We lived."

1939

ISTANBUL HOUSE OF DETENTION

In the Istanbul Detention House yard
on a sunny winter day after rain,
as clouds, red tiles, walls, and my face
                    trembled in puddles on the ground,
I—with all that was bravest and meanest in me,
strongest and weakest—
I thought of the world, my country, and you.

1
My love,
they're on the march:
heads forward, eyes wide open,
the red glare of burning cities,
                crops trampled,
                endless
                      footsteps.
And people slaughtered:
                like trees and calves,
                only easier
                    and faster.

My love,
amid these footsteps and this slaughter
I sometimes lost my freedom, bread, and you,
but never my faith in the days that will come
out of the darkness, screams, and hunger,
knocking on our door with hands full of sun.

2
I'm wonderfully happy I came into the world:
I love its earth, light, struggle, bread.

Although I know its dimensions from pole to pole
                          to the centimeter,
and while I'm not unaware it's a mere toy next to the sun,
the world for me is unbelievably big.
I would have liked to go around the world
and see the fish, fruits, and stars I haven't seen.
However,
I made my European trip only in books and pictures.
In my whole life I never got one letter
                with its blue stamp canceled in Asia.
Me and our corner grocer,
we're both mightily unknown in America.
Nevertheless,
from China to Spain, from the Cape of Good Hope to Alaska,
in every nautical mile, in every kilometer, I have friends
                                    and enemies.
Such friends that we haven't met even once
yet we can die for the same bread, the same freedom, the same
    dream.
And such enemies that they thirst for my blood—
                          I thirst for theirs.
My strength
is that I'm not alone in this big world.
The world and its people are no secret in my heart,
                no mystery in my science.
Calmly and openly
            I took my place
                          in the great struggle.
And without it,
            you and the earth
                  are not enough for me.
And yet you are astonishingly beautiful,
            the earth is warm and beautiful.

3

I love my country:
I've swung on its plane trees,
I've slept in its prisons.
Nothing lifts my spirits like its songs and tobacco.

My country:
Bedreddin, Sinan, Yunus Emré, and Sakarya,
lead domes and factory chimneys—
it's all the work of my people, whose drooping mustaches
hide their smiles
even from themselves.

My country:
so big
it seems endless.
Edirné, Izmir, Ulukishla, Marash, Trabzon, Erzurum.
All I know of the Erzurum plateau are its songs,
and I'm ashamed to say
I never crossed the Tauruses
to visit the cotton pickers
                              in the south.

My country:
camels, trains, Fords, and sick donkeys,
poplars,
          willow trees,
                        and red earth.

My country:
goats on the Ankara plain,
the sheen of their long blond silky hair.
The succulent plump hazelnuts of Giresun.
Amasya apples with fragrant red cheeks,

olives,
  figs,
    melons,
and bunches and bunches of grapes
        all colors,
then plows
and black oxen,
and then my people,
  ready to embrace
    with the wide-eyed joy of children
anything modern, beautiful, and good—
my honest, hard-working, brave people,
  half full, half hungry,
      half slaves. . .

          February 1939

HELLO

Nazim, what happiness
that, open and confident,
you can say "Hello"
from the bottom of your heart!

The year is 1940.
The month, July.
The day is the first Thursday of the month.
The hour: 9.

Date your letters in detail this way.
We live in such a world
                that the month, day, and hour
                speak volumes.

Hello, everybody.

To say a big
                fat "Hello"
and then, without finishing my sentence,
                to look at you with a smile
—sly and gleeful—
                and wink. . .

We're such perfect friends
                that we understand each other
                        without words or writing. . .

Hello, everybody,
hello to all of you. . .

LETTERS FROM CHANKIRI PRISON

1
Four o'clock,
            no you.
Five o'clock,
            nothing.
Six, seven,
tomorrow,
the day after,
and maybe—
            who knows...

I had a garden
      in the prison yard.
About fifteen paces long,
      at the foot of a sunny wall.
You used to come,
and we'd sit side by side,
your big red
      oilcloth bag
                  on your knees...

Remember "Head" Mehmet?
From the juveniles ward.
Square head,
thick short legs,
and hands bigger than his feet.
With a rock he'd brained a guy
      whose hive he robbed of honey.
He used to call you "Good lady."
He had a garden smaller than mine
                  right above me,
                              nearer the sun,
                  in a tin can.

Do you remember a Saturday,
a late afternoon sprinkled
                    by the prison fountain?
The tinsmith Shaban sang a song,
remember:
          "Beypazari is my home, my city—
          who knows where I'll leave my body?"

I did so many pictures of you,
and you didn't leave me even one.
All I have is a photograph:
in another garden,
                    very at ease,
                    very happy,
          you're feeding some chickens
                    and laughing.

The prison garden didn't have any chickens,
but we could laugh all right
                    and we weren't unhappy.
How we heard news
                    of beautiful freedom,
how we listened for the footsteps
                    of good news coming,
what beautiful things we talked about
                    in the prison garden. . .

2
One afternoon
we sat
at the prison gate
and read Ghazali's rubaiyat:
"Night:
          the great azure garden.

The gold-spangled whirling of the dancers.
And the dead stretched out in their wooden boxes."

If one day,
far from me,
life weighs on you
like a dark rain,
        read Ghazali again.
And I know,
my Pirayé,
you'll feel only pity
for his desperate loneliness
                and awful dread
                of death.

Let flowing water bring Ghazali to you:
"The king is but an earthen bowl
        on the Potter's shelf,
and victories are told
        on the ruined walls of the king of kings."

Welling up and springing forth.
Cold
        hot
            cool.
And in the great azure garden,
                    the eternal
                    ceaseless turning
                    of the dancers.

I don't know why
I keep thinking
of a Chankiri saying
I first heard from you:

"When the poplars are in bloom,
                    cherries will come soon."
The poplars are blooming in Ghazali,
but
the master doesn't see
                    the cherries coming.
That's why he worships death.

Upstairs, "Sugar" Ali plays his music.
Evening.
Outside, everybody's shouting.
Water is flowing from the fountain.
And in the light of the guardhouse,
tied to the acacias, three baby wolves.
Beyond the bars
        my great azure garden opens up.
W h a t   i s   r e a l   i s   l i f e . . .

Don't forget me, Pirayé...

3
Wednesday today—
you know,
Chankiri's market day.
Its eggs and bulgur,
its gilded purple eggplants,
will even reach us,
passing through our iron door in reed baskets...

Yesterday
I watched them come down from the villages
tired,
wily,
        and suspicious,

with sorrow under their brows.
They passed by—the men on donkeys,
the women on bare feet.
You probably know some of them.
And the last two Wednesdays they probably missed
          the red-scarfed, "not-uppity"
          lady from Istanbul. . .

20 July 1940

4
The heat is like nothing you've ever known,
and I who grew up by the sea—
the sea is so far away. . .

Between two and five
I lie under the mosquito net
—soaking wet,
motionless,
eyes open—
and listen to the flies buzz.
I know
in the yard now
they're splashing water on the walls,
steam rising from the hot red stones.
And outside, skirting the burnt grass
of the fortress, the black-
bricked city sits
in nitric acid light. . .

Nights a wind comes up suddenly
and suddenly dies.
And the heat, panting like a beast
in the dark, moves on soft furry feet,

threatening me with something.
And from time to time
I shiver in my skin,
          afraid of nature...

There may be an earthquake.
It's just three days away.
The danger rocked Yozgat.
And the people here say:
because it sits on a salt mine,
        Chankiri will collapse
            forty days before doomsday.
To go to bed one night
and not wake up in the morning,
        your head smashed by a wooden beam.
What a blind, good-for-nothing death.
I want to live a little longer,
a good deal longer.
I want this for many things,
for many
very important things.

12 August 1940

5
It gets dark at five
with clouds on the attack.
They clearly carry rain.
Many
pass low enough to touch.
The hundred watts in my room
and the tailors' oil lamps are lit.
The tailors are drinking linden tea...
Which means winter's here...

I'm cold.
But not sad.
This privilege is reserved for us:
on winter days in prison,
and not just in prison
but in the big world
      that should
         and will
            be warm,
                  to be cold
                  but not sad...

26 October 1940

A STRANGE FEELING

"The plum trees
         are in bloom
—the wild apricot flowers first,
               the plum last. . .

My love,
let's sit
knee to knee
on the grass.
The air is delicious and light
—but not really warm yet—
and the almonds are green
              and fuzzy, still
                  very soft. . .

We're happy
         because we're alive.
We'd probably have been killed long ago
if you were in London,
if I were in Tobruk or on an English freighter. . .

Put your hands on your knees, my love
—your wrists thick and white—
and open your left hand:
the daylight is inside your palm
            like an apricot. . .
Of the people dead in yesterday's air raid,
         about a hundred were under five,
twenty-four still babies. . .

I like the color of pomegranate seeds, my love
—a pomegranate seed, seed of light—
I like melons fragrant,
my plums tart. . ."

... a rainy day
far from fruits and you
—not a single tree has bloomed yet,
and there's even a chance of snow—
in Bursa Prison,
carried away by a strange feeling
and about to explode,
I write this out of pigheadedness
—out of sheer spite—for myself and the people I love.

7 February 1941

ON THE TWENTIETH CENTURY

"To sleep
          and wake a hundred years later, my love . . . "

"No,
          my century doesn't scare me.
                         I'm not a deserter.
My miserable,
          shameful century,
my daring,
          great,
                    heroic century.
I've never regretted I was born too soon.
I'm proud to be
a child of the twentieth century.
I'm satisfied
          to join its ranks
                    on our side
and fight for a new world . . . "

"A hundred years later, my love . . . "

"No, in spite of everything, *earlier.*
And my dying, dawning century
when those who laugh last will laugh best
—my awful night that comes to light with rising cries—
will be all sunshine,
          like your eyes . . . "

12 November 1941

LETTER FROM MY WIFE

I
want to die before you.
Do you think the one who follows
finds the one who went first?
I don't think so.
It would be best to have me burned
and put in a jar
            over your fireplace.
Make the jar
clear glass,
            so you can watch me inside. . .
You see my sacrifice:
I give up being earth,
I give up being a flower,
                        just to stay near you.
And I become dust
to live with you.
Then, when you die,
you can come into my jar
and we'll live there together,
your ashes with mine,
until some dizzy bride
or wayward grandson
tosses us out. . .
But
by then
we'll be
so mixed
together
that even at the dump our atoms
                        will fall side by side.
We'll dive into the earth together.
And if one day a wild flower

finds water and springs from that piece of earth,
its stem will have
two blooms for sure:
> one will be you,
> the other me.

I'm not
about to die yet.
I want to bear another child.
I'm full of life.
My blood is hot.
I'll live a long, long time—
with you.
Death doesn't scare me,
I just don't find our funeral arrangements
> too attractive.
But everything could change
before I die.
Any chance you'll get out of prison soon?
Something inside me says:
> *Maybe.*

18 February 1945

9-10 P.M. POEMS

How beautiful to think of you:
amid news of death and victory,
in prison,
when I'm past forty...

How beautiful to think of you:
your hand resting on blue cloth,
your hair grave and soft
like my beloved Istanbul earth...
The joy of loving you
        is like a second person inside me...
The smell of geranium leaves on my fingers,
a sunny quiet,
and the call of flesh:
        a warm
                deep darkness
                        parted by bright red lines...

How beautiful to think of you,
to write about you,
to sit back in prison and remember you:
what you said on this or that day in such and such a place,
                        not the words themselves
                        but the world in their aura...

How beautiful to think of you.
I must carve you something from wood—
                        a box,
                                a ring—
and weave you about three meters of fine silk.
And jumping
        right up
and grabbing the iron bars at my window,

I must shout out the things I write for you
                  to the milk-white blue of freedom...

How beautiful to think of you:
amid news of death and victory,
in prison,
when I'm past forty...

20 September 1945

At this late hour
this fall night
            I am full of your words:
words
      eternal like time and matter,
           naked like eyes,
                heavy like hands,
      and bright like stars.

Your words came
from your heart, flesh, and mind.
They brought you:
            mother,
                wife,
                    and friend.
They were sad, painful, happy, hopeful, brave—
                your words were *human*...

21 September 1945

Our son is sick,
his father's in prison,
your head is heavy in your tired hands:
our fate is like the world's...

People bring better days,
our son gets well,
his father comes out of prison,
your gold eyes smile:
our fate is like the world's...

22 September 1945

I read a book,
                you are in it;
I hear a song,
                you're in it.
I eat my bread,
                    you're sitting facing me;
I work,
        and you sit watching me.
You who are everywhere my "Ever Present,"
                        I cannot talk with you,
                            we cannot hear each other's voice:
you are my eight-year widow...

23 September 1945

What is she doing now,
            right now, this instant?
Is she in the house or outside?
Is she working, lying down, or standing up?
Maybe she's just raised her arm—
hey,
        how this suddenly bares her thick white wrist!

What is she doing now,
            right now, this instant?

Maybe she's petting
                    a kitten on her lap.
Or maybe she's walking, about to take a step—
those beloved feet that take her straight to me
                              on my dark days!
And what's she thinking about—
                         me?
Or—
      oh, I don't know—
                        why the beans refuse to cook?
Or else
        why most people are this unhappy?

What is she doing now,
              right now, this instant?

24 September 1945

The most beautiful sea
                   hasn't been crossed yet.
The most beautiful child
                   hasn't grown up yet.
Our most beautiful days
                we haven't seen yet.
And the most beautiful words I wanted to tell you
                   I haven't said yet...

25 September 1945

Nine o'clock.
The bell struck in the town square,
the ward doors will close any minute.
Prison has lasted a bit long this time:
                              eight years...

Living is a matter of hope, my love.
Living
　　　　is a serious business, like loving you...

26 September 1945

They've taken us prisoner,
they've locked us up:
　　　　　me inside the walls,
　　　　　　　you outside.
But that's nothing.
The worst
is when people—knowingly or not—
carry prison inside themselves...
Most people have been forced to do this,
honest, hard-working, good people
who deserve to be loved as much as I love you...

30 September 1945

Thinking of you is beautiful
　　　　　　　　and hopeful,
like listening to the best voice in the world
　　　　　sing the loveliest song.
But hope is not enough for me:
I no longer want to listen,
　　　　　　　I want to sing the songs...

1 October 1945

Over the mountain:
a cloud flush with evening sun over the mountain.

Today, too:
today, too, passed without you—I mean, without half the world.
Soon they'll open
red on red:
soon the four-o'clocks will open red on red.
In the air, brave soundless wings bridge
　　　　our separation, which feels like exile...

2 October 1945

The wind blows on, the same cherry branch
doesn't bend in the same wind even once.
Birds chirp in the tree:
　　　　　　　　the wings want to fly.
The door is closed:
　　　　　　　　it wants to break open.
I want you:
life should be
beautiful like you,
　　　　friendly and loving...
I know the feast of poverty
　　　　　　　still isn't over...
It will be yet...

5 October 1945

We both know, my love,
they taught us:
　　　　how to be hungry, cold,
　　　　tired to death,
　　　　and apart.
We haven't been forced to kill yet
or to go through the business of being killed.

We both know, my love,
we can teach:
    how to fight for our people
    and how—a little better
          and deeper each day—
                  to love...

6 October 1945

Clouds pass, heavy with news.
The letter that didn't come crumples in my hand.
My heart is at the tips of my eyelashes,
    blessing the earth that disappears into the distance.
I want to call out: "P i r a y é ,
          P i r a y é !"

7 October 1945

At night human cries
          cross the open sea
               with the winds.
It's not safe yet
    to sail the open sea at night...

The fields haven't been plowed for six years—
tank treads still track the earth.
Snow
    will bury the tank tracks this winter.

Ah, light of my life,
the antennas are lying again
so the merchants of sweat can close their books
        with a hundred-percent profit.

But those back from feasting at Azrael's table
                    have come back with sealed fates. . .

8 October 1945

    I've become impossible again:
                    sleepless, irritable, perverse.
    One day
            I work
as if beating a wild beast, as if cursing all that's holy,
    and the next day
I lie on my back from morning to night,
    a lazy song on my lips like an unlit cigarette.
    And it drives me crazy,
                    the hatred
                            and pity I feel for myself. . .

    I've become impossible again:
                    sleepless, irritable, perverse.
    Again, as always, I'm wrong.
    I have no cause
                    and couldn't possibly.
    What I'm doing is shameful,
                    a disgrace.
    But I can't help it:
                    I'm jealous of you,
                        forgive me. . .

9 October 1945

Last night I saw you in a dream:
sitting at my knee, you raised your head
and looked at me with your big gold eyes.

104

You asked something.
Your moist lips opened and closed,
                    but I couldn't hear your voice.

Somewhere in the night a clock rang out like good news.
The air whispered of infinity.
I heard "Memo"—my canary—singing in his red cage,
the crackle of seeds pushing through a plowed field,
and the righteous, triumphant hum of a crowd.
Your moist lips still opened and closed,
                         but I couldn't hear your voice . . .

I woke up broken.
I had fallen asleep over a book.
I thought:
         Were all those sounds your voice?

10 October 1945

When I look into your eyes
          the smell of sunny earth hits me:
          I'm in a wheat field, lost amid the grain.

Their bottomless green-glittering abyss
is ever-changing like eternal matter,
          which is forever giving up its secrets
          but will never
          totally surrender . . .

18 October 1945

As I go forth from the castle door to meet death,
my love, I can say

to the city I see for the last time:
      "Although you didn't make me all that happy,
      I did my best
                  to make you
                        happy.
      You continue on your way to happiness,
                        life continues.
      I'm at peace,
      my heart satisfied with earning your bread,
      my eyes sad to be leaving your light.
                        I came and here I go—
                        be of good cheer, Aleppo. . ."

27 October 1945

We are one half of an apple,
                  the other half is this big world.
We are one half of an apple,
                  the other half is our people.
You are one half of an apple,
                  the other half is me,
                              us two. . .

28 October 1945

The swelling fragrance of the rose geranium,
the humming of the sea,
and fall is here with its full clouds and wise earth. . .

My love,
the years have ripened.
We've gone through so much
      we could be a thousand years old.

But we are still
> wide-eyed children
>   > running barefoot in the sun, hand in hand...

5 November 1945

Forget the flowering almonds.
They aren't worth it:
in this business
> what cannot come back should not be remembered.
Dry your hair in the sun:
> let the wet, heavy reds
>   > glow with the languor of ripe fruit...
My love, my love,
> the season
>   >   fall...

8 November 1945

Over the rooftops of my far-off city
under the Sea of Marmara
and across the fall earth
>   > your voice came
>   >   > rich and liquid.
For three minutes.
Then the phone went black...

12 November 1945

The last south winds blow warm,
> humming like blood spurting from an artery.
I listen to the air:
>   > the pulse has slowed.

There's snow on Mount Uludagh,
and on Cherry Hill the bears have gone to sleep
                on red chestnut leaves, cuddly and grand.
The poplars are undressing on the plain.
The silkworm eggs are moved inside for the winter,
fall is almost over,
the earth is sinking into its pregnant sleep.
And we will pass another winter
                in our great anger,
                warmed by the fire of our sacred hope. . .

13 November 1945

The poverty of Istanbul—they say—defies description,
hunger—they say—has ravaged the people,
TB—they say—is everywhere.
Little girls this high—they say—
                in burned-out buildings, movie theaters. . .

Dark news comes from my far-off city
of honest, hard-working, poor people—
                                the real Istanbul,
which is your home, my love,
and which I carry in the bag on my back
        wherever I'm exiled, to whatever prison,
        the city I hold in my heart like the loss of a child,
        like your image in my eyes. . .

20 November 1945

Though an occasional carnation still blooms in the flowerpots,
the fall plowing is over on the plain:
                they're sowing seeds now.

And picking olives.
Both moving into winter
and making way for the spring shoots.
And me, full of you
        and weighed down with the impatience of great journeys,
        I lie in Bursa like an anchored freighter...

4 December 1945

Take out the dress I first saw you in,
look your best,
look like spring trees...
Wear in your hair
        the carnation I sent you in a letter from prison,
raise your kissable, lined, broad white forehead.
Today, not broken and sad—
                        no way!—
today Nazim Hikmet's woman must be beautiful
                like a rebel flag...

5 December 1945

The keel has snapped,
the slaves are breaking their chains.
That's a northeaster blowing,
it'll smash the hull on the rocks.
This world, this pirate ship, will sink—
                come hell or high water, it will sink.
And we will build a world as hopeful, free,
                and open as your forehead, my Pirayé...

6 December 1945

They are the enemies of hope, my love,
of flowing water
   and the fruitful tree,
   of life growing and unfolding.
Death has branded them—
      rotting teeth, decaying flesh—
      and soon they will be dead and gone for good.
And yes, my love,
freedom will walk around swinging its arms
in its Sunday best—workers' overalls!—
      yes, freedom in this beautiful country. . .

7 December 1945

They're the enemy of Rejeb, the towel man in Bursa,
of the fitter Hassan in the Karabuk factory,
of the poor peasant woman Hatijé,
of the day laborer Suleiman,
they're your enemy and mine,
the enemy of anyone who thinks,
and this country, the home of these people—
my love, they're the enemy of this country. . .

12 December 1945

The trees on the plain make one last effort to shine:
     spangled gold
       copper
         bronze and wood. . .
The oxen's hooves sink softly into the moist earth.

110

And the mountains are plunged in fog:
                    lead-gray, soaking wet...
That's it—
fall must be finally over today.
Wild geese just shot by,
                    probably headed for Iznik Lake.
The air is cool
        and smells like soot:
        the smell of snow is in the air.

To be outside now,
        to ride a horse at full gallop toward the mountains...
You'll say, "You don't know how to ride a horse,"
but don't laugh
        or get jealous:
I've picked up a new habit in prison,
I love nature nearly as much
                    as I love you.
                    And both of you are far away...

13 December 1945

Snow came on suddenly at night.
Morning was crows exploding from white branches.
Winter on the Bursa plain as far as the eye can see:
a world without end.
My love,
the season's changed
        in one leap after great labor.
And under the snow, proud
                    hard-working life
                        continues...

14 December 1945

Damn it, winter has come down hard. . .
You and my honest Istanbul, who knows how you are?
Do you have coal?
Could you buy wood?
Line the windows with newspaper.
Go to bed early.
Probably nothing's left in the house to sell.
To be cold and half hungry:
        here, too, we're the majority
        in the world, our country, and our city. . .

NINTH ANNIVERSARY

One night of knee-deep snow
my adventure started—
pulled from the supper table,
thrown into a police car,
packed off on a train,
and locked up in a room.
Its ninth year ended three days ago.

In the corridor a man on a stretcher
is dying open-mouthed on his back,
the grief of long iron years in his face.

I think of isolation,
        sickening and total,
                like that of the mad and the dead:
first, seventy-six days
        of the silent hostility of a closed door,
then seven weeks in the hold of a ship.
Still, I wasn't defeated:
my head
        was a second person at my side.

I've forgotten most of their faces
—all I remember is a very long pointed nose—
yet how many times they lined up before me!
When my sentence was read, they had one worry:
                        to look imposing.
                        They did not.
They looked more like things than people:
like wall clocks, stupid
        and arrogant,
and sad and pathetic like handcuffs, chains, etc.

A city without houses or streets.
Tons of hope, tons of grief.
The distances microscopic.
Of the four-legged creatures, just cats.

I live in a world of forbidden things!
To smell your lover's cheek:
                    forbidden.
To eat at the same table with your children:
                                forbidden.
To talk with your brother or your mother
    without a wire screen or a guard between you:
                                forbidden.
To seal a letter you've written
or to get a letter still sealed:
                    forbidden.
To turn off the light when you go to bed:
                            forbidden.
To play backgammon:
            forbidden.
And not that it isn't forbidden,
    but what you can hide in your heart and have in your hand
        is to love, think, and understand.

In the corridor the man on the stretcher died.
They took him away.
Now no hope, no grief,
            no bread, no water,
            no freedom, no prison,
            no wanting women, no guards, no bedbugs,
            and no more cats to sit and stare at him.
                That business is finished, over.

But mine goes on:
my head keeps loving, thinking, understanding,
my impotent rage goes on eating me,
and, since morning, my liver goes on aching. . .

20 January 1946

HAZEL ARE MY LADY'S EYES

Hazel are my lady's eyes,
with waves and waves of green—
gold leaf overlaid with green moiré.
Brothers, what's the story?
For nine years our hands haven't touched:
I got old here,
she there.

My girl, your thick white neck is lined,
but we can't possibly get old
—we need another term for sagging flesh—
because people are old
only if they love no one but themselves.

1947

RUBAIYAT

First Series

1

The world you saw was real, Rumi, not an apparition, etc.
It is boundless and eternal, its painter is not the First Cause, etc.
And the best of the rubaiyat your burning flesh left us
is not the one that goes, "All forms are shadows," etc....

2

My soul neither was before she was, nor attains to a mystery that
                                                            isn't she:
my soul is an image of her, she the image of the outside world
                                                    reflected in me.
And the image farthest from and closest to its original
is my love's beauty illuminating me...

3

My love's image in the mirror had its say:
"She is not—I am," it said to me one day.
I struck, the mirror broke, the image disappeared
but, thank goodness, my love stays...

4

I painted you on canvas only once
but picture you a thousand times a day.
Amazingly, your image there will last:
canvas has a longer life than I...

5

I can't kiss or make love to your image,
but there in my city you're flesh and blood,
and your red mouth, the honey I'm denied, your big eyes, really are,
and your surrender like rebel waters, your whiteness I can't even
                                                            touch...

6

She kissed me: "These lips are real like the universe," she said.
"This fragrance isn't your invention, it's the spring in my hair,"
                                                          she said.
"Watch them in the sky or in my eyes:
the blind may not see them, but the stars are there," she said . . .

7

This garden, this moist earth, this jasmine scent, this moonlit
                                                          night
will sparkle still when I've passed from the light,
because it was before I came, and afterwards wasn't part of me—
a mere copy of this original appeared in me . . .

8

One day Mother Nature will say, "Quitting time—
          no more laughter or tears, my child . . ."
And endless once again it will begin:
          life that doesn't see, speak, or think . . .

9

Each day separation draws closer:
good-bye, my beautiful world,
and hello,
          u n i v e r s e . . .

10

Full honeycomb—
I mean, your eyes full of sun . . .
Your eyes, my love, will be dust tomorrow,
the honey will fill other combs . . .

11
They're neither
              light nor clay,
my love, her cat, and the bead on his collar:
it's all in the kneading, the dough is the same . . .

12
Cabbage, car, plague germ, star:
we're all kith and kin.
Not *"Cogito ergo sum,"* my sun-eyed love,
but, in this distinguished family, we think because we are . . .

13
Between us just a difference of degree—
that's how it is, my canary:
you an unthinking bird, with wings,
and me with hands, a man who thinks . . .

Second Series

1
"Fill your cup with wine before your cup fills with dust," said
                                        Khayyam.
A man with a bony nose and no shoes stared at him in his rose
                                        garden:
"In this world with more blessings than stars," the man said,
                                        "I'm starving,
I don't have enough money to buy bread, let alone wine . . ."

2

To think with sweet sorrow on death and life's brevity,
to drink wine in the tulip garden by moonlight...
We never felt this sweet sorrow our whole life
in the basement of a coal-black house in Edge City...

3

Life is passing—seize time's bounty before you sleep the unwaking sleep:
fill the crystal goblet with ruby wine—young man, it's dawn, awake...
In his bare, ice-cold room the young man woke to the shriek
of the factory whistle, which didn't forgive being late...

4

I don't miss days gone by
      —except one summer night—
and even the last blue sparkle of my eyes
      will flash you news of days to come...

5

Me, one man, the Turkish poet
Nazim Hikmet,
I'm faith from head to toe—
from head to toe, struggle and hope...

6

I, the announcer, speak,
my voice somber and naked as a seed:
I'm setting the time of my heart,
at the tone it will be dawn...

Third Series

1
Either people love you
or they're your enemy.
Either you're forgotten as if you didn't exist,
or you're not out of mind even a minute . . .

2
Clear as glass, an unspoiled winter day—
to bite into the firm white flesh of a healthy apple!
My love, it's like the joy of breathing
in a snowy pine forest, this loving you . . .

3
Who knows, we might not have loved each other so
if we couldn't watch each other from afar.
Who knows, if fate hadn't torn us apart
we might never have been so close . . .

4
Night pales, day breaks.
Like water settling, everything grows clear, transparent.
My love, it's as if we suddenly came face to face:
all I see is light, light . . .

Fourth Series

1
To fight lies in the heart, in books, and on the street,
in mothers' lullabies and the announcer's news;
to know—my love, it's a great happiness—
to know what's been and what's to be . . .

2
Our arms are branches heavy with fruit:
the enemy shakes and shakes us,
and the better to harvest our fruit
they don't chain our feet but fetter our heads...

3
As long as you love
and love as much as you can,
as long as you give your all to your love
and give as much as you can, you are young...

4
I think of Yahya Kemal, the Ottomans' poet laureate:
I see him in a store window, looking fat and pained.
And for some reason I suddenly think
of lame Byron dying in the Greek mountains...

5
I am a patient gardener,
you are my rose that blooms every seven years.
I don't lose heart because you are so rare—
I think that may be why you are so dear...

6
In this business you must be hard and a little proud:
not cruelty, grief, or sorrow
but death alone
                must see you surrender...

7
I don't mean to boast but
I've shot through ten years of bondage like a bullet.
And the pain in my liver aside,
my heart is still the same heart, my head still the same head...

SINCE I WAS THROWN INSIDE

Since I was thrown inside
    the earth has gone around the sun ten times.
If you ask it:
        "That's nothing—
            a microscopic span."
If you ask me:
        "Ten years of my life!"
I had a pencil
    the year I was thrown inside.
It lasted me a week.
If you ask it:
        "A whole lifetime!"
If you ask me:
        "What's a week?"

Since I've been inside
    Osman did his seven-and-a-half
        for manslaughter and left,
        knocked around on the outside for a while,
        then landed back inside for smuggling,
        served six months, and got out again;
        yesterday we had a letter—he's married,
        with a kid coming in the spring.

They're ten years old now
    the children born
        the year I was thrown inside.
And that year's foals, shaky on their spindly long legs,
    have been wide-rumped, contented mares for some time.
But the olive seedlings are still saplings,
        still children.

New squares have opened in my far-off city
                    since I was thrown inside.
And my family now lives
        in a house I haven't seen
                    on a street I don't know.

Bread was like cotton, soft and white,
                    the year I was thrown inside.
Then it was rationed,
and here inside men killed
                    for a fist-sized black loaf.

Now it's free again
but dark and tasteless.

The year I was thrown inside
        the SECOND hadn't started yet.

The ovens at Dachau hadn't been lit,
nor the atom bomb dropped on Hiroshima.

Time flowed like blood from a child's slit throat.
Then that chapter was officially closed.
Now the American dollar talks of a THIRD.

Still, the day has gotten lighter
                    since I was thrown inside.
And "at the edge of darkness,
        pushing against the earth with their heavy hands,
                    THEY've risen up" halfway.

Since I was thrown inside
        the earth has gone around the sun ten times.
And I repeat with the same passion
        what I wrote about THEM
                    the year I was thrown inside:

"They who are numberless like ants in the earth,
                                fish in the sea,
                                        birds in the air,
who are cowardly, brave,
                ignorant, wise,
                                and childlike,
and who destroy
        and create,
my songs tell only of their adventures."
                        And anything else,
                                such as my ten years here,
                                        is just so much talk.

1947

I LOVE YOU

I kneel down: I look at the earth,
the grass,
insects,
little stems blooming with blues.
You are like the spring earth, my love,
                    I'm looking at you.

I lie on my back: I see the sky,
the branches of a tree,
storks on the wing,
a waking dream.
You are like the spring sky, my love,
                    I see you.

At night I light a campfire: I touch fire,
water,
cloth,
silver.
You are like a fire lit beneath the stars,
                    I touch you.

I go among people: I love people,
action,
thought,
struggle.
You are one person in my struggle,
                    I love you.

1947

ON IBRAHIM BALABAN'S PAINTING "SPRING"

Here, eyes, see Balaban's art.
Here is dawn: the month is May.
Here is light:
                        smart, brave, fresh, alive, pitiless.
Here are clouds:
                        like whipped cream.
Here, mountains:
                        cool and blue.
Here are foxes on their morning rounds—
light on their long tails,
        alarm on their pointed noses.
Here, eyes, look:
hungry, hairs raised, red-mouthed,
here on a mountaintop, a wolf.
Haven't you ever felt
the rage of a hungry wolf at sunrise?
Here, eyes, see: butterflies, bees,
the flash of sparkling fish.
Here, a stork
                        just back from Egypt.
Here is a deer,
                        creature of a more beautiful world.
Here, eyes, see the bear outside its den,
                                still sleepy.
Haven't you ever thought of living
unconsciously like bears, sniffing the earth,
close to pears and the mossy dark,
far from human voices and fire?
Here, eyes, look: squirrels, rabbits,
lizards, turtles,
our grape-eyed donkey.
Here, eyes, see
a shimmering tree,

most like a person in its beauty.
Here is green grass:
                    go ahead, my bare feet.
Here, nose, smell:
                    mint, thyme.
Here, mouth, water:
                    sorrels, mallows.
Touch, hands, caress, hold—
here, my mother's milk,
      my wife's flesh,
           my child's smile.
Here is plowed earth,
here is man:
lord of rocks and mountains, the birds and the beasts.
Here are his sandals, here the patches on his breeches.
Here is the plow,
and here are the oxen with sad, terrible sores on their rumps.

1947

128

ABOUT MOUNT ULUDAGH

For seven years now Uludagh and I
    have stared each other in the eye.
It hasn't budged an inch
    and neither have I,
yet we know each other well.
Like anything living, it can laugh and get mad.

Sometimes
    in winter, especially at night,
        when the wind blows from the south,
with its snowy pine forests, plateaus, and frozen lakes
    it rolls over in its sleep,
and the Old Man who lives way at the top
    —long beard flying,
            skirts billowing—
rides the howling wind down into the valley...

Then sometimes,
    especially in May, at sunup,
    it rises like a brand-new world—
        huge, blue, vast,
        free and happy.

Then there are days
    it looks like its picture on the pop bottles.
And in its hotel I can't see, I know
        lady skiers sipping cognac
        are flirting with the gentleman skiers.

And the day arrives
when one of its beetle-browed mountain folk, having
butchered his neighbor at the altar of sacred property,
     comes to us like a guest in his yellow homespun trousers
        to do fifteen years in Cell Block 71.

1947

THE STRANGEST CREATURE ON EARTH

You're like a scorpion, my brother,
you live in cowardly darkness
              like a scorpion.
You're like a sparrow, my brother,
always in a sparrow's flutter.
You're like a clam, my brother,
closed like a clam, content.
And you're scary, my brother,
              like the mouth of a sleeping volcano.

Not one,
       not five—
sadly, you number millions.
You're like a sheep, my brother:
              when the cloaked drover raises his stick,
                     you quickly join the flock
and run, almost proudly, to the slaughterhouse.
I mean, you're the strangest creature on earth—
even stranger than the fish
              that couldn't see the ocean for the water.
And the oppression in this world
              is thanks to you.
And if we're hungry, tired, covered with blood,
and still being crushed like grapes for our wine,
                     the fault is yours—
I can hardly bring myself to say it,
but most of the fault, my dear brother, is yours.

1947

131

ON LIVING

I

Living is no laughing matter:
    you must live with great seriousness
        like a squirrel, for example—
  I mean, without looking for something beyond and above living,
      I mean living must be your whole life.
Living is no laughing matter:
    you must take it seriously,
      so much so and to such a degree
    that, for example, your hands tied behind your back,
                          your back to the wall,
or else in a laboratory
    in your white coat and safety glasses,
    you can die for people—
even for people whose faces you've never seen,
even though you know living
    is the most real, the most beautiful thing.
I mean, you must take living so seriously
    that even at seventy, for example, you'll plant olive trees—
    and not for your children, either,
    but because although you fear death you don't believe it,
    because living, I mean, weighs heavier.

II

Let's say we're seriously ill, need surgery—
which is to say we might not get up
            from the white table.
Even though it's impossible not to feel sad
         about going a little too soon,
we'll still laugh at the jokes being told,

we'll look out the window to see if it's raining,
or still wait anxiously
               for the latest newscast. . .
Let's say we're at the front—
               for something worth fighting for, say.
There, in the first offensive, on that very day,
       we might fall on our face, dead.
We'll know this with a curious anger,
       but we'll still worry ourselves to death
       about the outcome of the war, which could last years.
Let's say we're in prison
and close to fifty,
and we have eighteen more years, say,
               before the iron doors will open.
We'll still live with the outside,
with its people and animals, struggle and wind—
               I mean with the outside beyond the walls.
I mean, however and wherever we are,
       we must live as if we will never die.

III

This earth will grow cold,
a star among stars
               and one of the smallest,
a gilded mote on blue velvet—
       I mean *this,* our great earth.
This earth will grow cold one day,
not like a block of ice
or a dead cloud even
but like an empty walnut it will roll along
               in pitch-black space. . .

You must grieve for this right now
—you have to feel this sorrow now—
for the world must be loved this much
                    if you're going to say "I lived"...

February 1948

IT'S THIS WAY

I stand in the advancing light,
my hands hungry, the world beautiful.

My eyes can't get enough of the trees—
they're so hopeful, so green.

A sunny road runs through the mulberries,
I'm at the window of the prison infirmary.

I can't smell the medicines—
carnations must be blooming nearby.

It's this way:
being captured is beside the point,
the point is not to surrender.

1948

ANGINA PECTORIS

If half my heart is here, doctor,
    the other half is in China
with the army flowing
    toward the Yellow River.
And every morning, doctor,
every morning at sunrise my heart
    is shot in Greece.
And every night, doctor,
when the prisoners are asleep and the infirmary is deserted,
my heart stops at a run-down old house
                    in Istanbul.
And then after ten years
all I have to offer my poor people
is this apple in my hand, doctor,
one red apple:
         my heart.
And that, doctor, that is the reason
for this angina pectoris—
not nicotine, prison, or arteriosclerosis.
I look at the night through the bars,
and despite the weight on my chest
my heart still beats with the most distant stars.

April 1948

OCCUPATION

As dawn breaks on the horns of my ox,
I plow the earth with patient pride.
The earth is moist and warm on my bare feet.

I beat iron all morning—
the darkness is dyed red.

In the afternoon heat I pick olives,
the leaves the loveliest of greens:
I'm light from head to toe.

Guests come without fail each evening,
my door is wide open
                      to all songs.

At night I wade knee-deep into the water
and pull the nets out of the sea:
the fish get all mixed up with the stars.

Now I'm responsible
                      for the state of the world:
people and earth, darkness and light.

So you see I'm up to my ears in work.
Hush, my rose, hush—
I'm busy falling in love with you.

1948

YOU'RE

You're my bondage and my freedom,
my flesh burning like a naked summer night,
you're my country.

Hazel eyes marbled green,
you're awesome, beautiful, and brave,
you're my desire always just out of reach.

I MADE A JOURNEY

Far off in the night,
    airport lights burned into the sky
like white flames,
and the trains I missed dived sparkling into the darkness,
    taking part of me away.
I made a journey.

I made a journey.
People's eyes were all white,
the putrid waters stank.
I passed through the swamp of lies and stupidity
    without getting lost in the head-high reeds . . .

I made a journey
with women sitting doubled over,
    their fists pressed to their flat bellies,
or running barefooted before the wind;
with the dead;
with those forgotten on battlefields and barricades.

I made a journey,
riding on trucks
    carrying prisoners
        through cities,
            the asphalt moist in the morning light . . .

I made a journey—
I couldn't get enough of the grapes crushed by your white teeth,
or your bed like a shuttered summer afternoon.

I made a journey:
brand-new buildings waited in warehouses,
hope shone bright green like a young pine,

and lamps blazed on foreheads
a thousand meters underground.

I made a journey
under the moon,
in the light of the sun and rain,
with the four seasons and all time,
with insects, grass, and stars,
and with the most honest people on earth—
I mean, affectionate like violins,
pitiless and brave
like children who can't talk yet,
ready to die as easily as birds
or live a thousand years...

1948

ABOUT YOUR HANDS AND LIES

Your hands grave like all stones,
sad like all prison songs,
clumsy and heavy like all beasts of burden,
your hands sullen like hungry children's faces.
Your hands nimble and light like bees,
full like breasts filled with milk,
brave like nature,
your hands hiding their soft touch under rough skin.

This world isn't balanced on a bull's horns—
                              it's in your hands.
People, my people,
they feed you lies.
But you're starving,
you need to be fed bread and meat.
And without one full meal at a white table,
you leave this world where fruits bend every branch.
Oh, my people,
especially in Asia, Africa,
        the Near and Middle East, Pacific islands,
                    and my countrymen
—I mean, more than seventy percent of all people—
you're old and absent-minded like your hands,
curious, amazed, and young like your hands.
Oh, my people,
my European, my American,
you're smart, bold, and forgetful like your hands—
like your hands, you're quick to seduce,
                    easy to deceive . . .

People, my people,
if the antennas lie,
if the presses lie,

if books lie,
if the posters on the walls and the ads in the columns lie,
if women's thighs naked on the silver screen lie,
if prayers,
lullabies,
and dreams lie,
if the fiddler at the tavern is lying,
if moonlight on the nights of hopeless days lies,
if voices lie,
and words,
if everyone and everything is lying
        but your hands,
it's so they'll be obedient like clay,
blind like darkness,
and dumb like sheep dogs—
it's so that your hands won't rebel.
And so that in this mortal, this livable world
        —where we're guests all too briefly anyway—
        this merchants' empire, this cruelty, won't end.

1949

SOME ADVICE TO THOSE WHO WILL SERVE TIME
IN PRISON

If instead of being hanged by the neck
        you're thrown inside
        for not giving up hope
in the world, your country, and people,
        if you do ten or fifteen years
        apart from the time you have left,
you won't say,
           "Better I had swung from the end of a rope
                  like a flag"—
you'll put your foot down and live.
It may not be a pleasure exactly,
but it's your solemn duty
      to live one more day
           to spite the enemy.
Part of you may live alone inside,
      like a stone at the bottom of a well.
But the other part
      must be so caught up
      in the flurry of the world
      that you shiver there inside
   when outside, at forty days' distance, a leaf moves.
To wait for letters inside,
to sing sad songs,
or to lie awake all night staring at the ceiling
         is sweet but dangerous.
Look at your face from shave to shave,
forget your age,
watch out for lice
        and for spring nights,
   and always remember
      to eat every last piece of bread—
also, don't forget to laugh heartily.

And who knows,
the woman you love may stop loving you.
Don't say it's no big thing:
it's like the snapping of a green branch
                              to the man inside.
To think of roses and gardens inside is bad,
to think of seas and mountains is good.
Read and write without rest,
and I also advise weaving
and making mirrors.
I mean, it's not that you can't pass
       ten or fifteen years inside
                              and more—
       you can,
       as long as the jewel
       on the left side of your chest doesn't lose its luster!

May 1949

144

ON THE MATTER OF ROMEO AND JULIET

It's no crime to be Romeo or Juliet;
it's not a crime even to die for love.
What counts is whether you can be a Romeo or Juliet—
I mean, it's all a question of your heart.

For instance, fighting at the barricades
or going off to explore the North Pole
or testing a new serum in your veins—
                    would it be a crime to die?

It's no crime to be Romeo or Juliet;
it's not a crime even to die for love.

You fall head over heels in love with the world,
but it doesn't know you're alive.
You don't want to leave the world,
but it will leave you—
I mean, just because you love apples,
do apples have to love you back?
I mean, if Juliet stopped loving Romeo
—or if she'd never loved him—
would he be any less a Romeo?

It's no crime to be Romeo or Juliet;
it's not a crime even to die for love.

1949

SADNESS

Is the sadness I feel
        these sunny winter days
        the longing to be somewhere else—
        on the bridge in my Istanbul, say,
        or with the workers in Adana
        or in the Greek mountains or in China,
        or beside her who no longer loves me?

Or is it a trick
                of my liver,
has a dream put me in this state,
or is it loneliness again
or the fact
            I'm pushing fifty?

The second chapter
of my sadness
        will tiptoe out
                and go the way it came—
        if I can just finish this poem
        or sleep a little better,
        if I just get a letter
        or some good news on the radio...

1949

ON IBRAHIM BALABAN'S PAINTING "THE PRISON GATES"

Six women wait outside the iron gates,
five squatting while one stands;

eight children wait outside the iron gates,
too young to even smile.

Six women wait outside the iron gates
with patient feet and grief-struck hands;

eight children wait outside the iron gates,
all swaddled infants with wide eyes.

Six women wait outside the iron gates,
their hair tucked out of sight;

eight children wait outside the iron gates,
one's hands clasped tight.

A guard stands outside the iron gates,
neither friend nor foe; his watch is long, the day hot.

There is a mule outside the iron gates:
it looks about to cry.

There is a dog outside the iron gates—
yellow, with a black nose.

There are straw baskets of green peppers, onions
and garlic in saddlebags, sacks of coal.

Six women wait outside the iron gates,
and inside—well, there are five hundred men;

you aren't one of the six women,
but I am one of the five hundred men.

28 December 1949
Bursa Prison

AFTER GETTING OUT OF PRISON

1. AWAKENING

You woke up.
Where are you?
At home.
You can't get used
        to waking up
        in your own house.
This is the kind of daze
        thirteen years of prison leaves you in.
Who's sleeping next to you?
It's not loneliness—it's your wife.
She's sleeping peacefully, like an angel.
Pregnancy becomes the lady.
What time is it?
Eight.
You're safe till night.
Because it's the custom:
        the police don't raid houses in broad daylight.

1950

2. THE EVENING WALK

You no sooner got out of prison
than you made your wife
            pregnant;
she's on your arm,
        and you're taking an evening walk
                around the neighborhood.
The lady's belly comes up to her nose.

She carries her sacred charge coyly;
you're respectful and proud.
The air is cool
like baby hands.
You want to hold it in your palms
and warm it up.
The neighborhood cats wait at the butcher's door,
and upstairs his curly-haired wife
has settled her breasts on the window sill,
watching the evening.
Half-light, spotless sky:
smack in the middle sits the evening star
sparkling like a glass of water.
Indian summer lasted long this year—
the mulberry trees are yellow,
but the figs are still green.
Refik the typesetter and the milkman Yorgi's middle daughter
go for an evening stroll,
their fingers locked.
The grocer Karabet's lights are on.
This Armenian citizen won't forgive
his father's slaughter in the Kurdish mountains.
But he likes you,
because you also can't forgive
those who blackened the Turkish people's name.
The tuberculars of the neighborhood and the shut-ins
peer out from behind glass.
The washwoman Huriyé's unemployed son
leaves for the coffeehouse
with a heavy heart.
Rahmi Bey's radio is giving the news:
in a country in the Far East,
moon-faced yellow people
are fighting a white dragon.
Of your people,

4500 Mehmets
          have been sent there to murder their brothers.
You blush
     with rage and shame
and not in general, either—
     this impotent grief
     is all yours.
It's as if they'd knocked your wife down from behind
                         and killed her child,
or you were back in prison
and they were making the peasant guards
                    beat the peasants again.

All of a sudden it's night.
The evening walk is over.
A police jeep turned into your street,
your wife whispered:
               "To our house?"

1950

3. ONE A.M.

Our books
—friendly, honest, and courageous—
are stacked up on the blue print tablecloth.
I've been freed from captivity,
          the enemy's fort in my own country.
It's one a.m.
We haven't turned off the light.
My wife lies next to me:
she's five months pregnant.
When my flesh touches hers,
when she lays my hand on her belly,
          the baby flutters.

A leaf on a branch,
    a fish in water,
        a child in the womb—
my child.
My child's mother knit
a pink baby shirt
a hand's-span wide—by my hand—
        with sleeves only this long.
If my child
is a girl, I want her to look like her mother
                from head to toe;
if a boy, tall like me.
If a girl, hazel-eyed;
a boy, true-blue.
My child.
Boy or girl,
I don't want my child to land in prison
            at any age
for standing up for beauty, justice, peace.
But, my son or daughter,
we know
if dawn is slow in lighting up the waters,
           you will fight
              and even...
Clearly, being a father here today
        is a pretty tough job.
It's one a.m.
We haven't turned off the light.
Maybe in half an hour or toward morning
my house will be raided again.
They might take me away,
        along with our books.
In the First Precinct's hands,
        I'll turn and look back:
my wife stands at the door,
        on the threshold,

her dress blowing in the morning wind.
In her full, heavy belly
   the baby flutters.

            1950

4. THE BIRTH

My wife bore me a little boy:
blond, no eyebrows,
wrapped in a blue blanket,
a ball of light weighing seven pounds.
When my son
     came into the world,
children were born in Korea
like yellow sunflowers.
MacArthur cut them down
before they'd had their fill of their mothers' milk.

When my son
     came into the world,
children were born in Greek prisons,
their fathers shot by firing squads.
The first thing they saw in this world
        were iron bars.
When my son
     came into the world,
children were born in Anatolia—
blue-eyed, black-eyed, hazel-eyed babies.
They got lice the minute they were born.
Who knows how many of them will survive by some miracle?
When my son
     reaches my age,
I won't be in this world,

but the world will be a wonderful cradle,
rocking
all children—
                black,
                        white,
                                and yellow—
on its globe-blue satin cushion.

1951

YOU

You are a field,
    I am the tractor.
You are paper,
    I am the typewriter.
My wife, mother of my son,
you are a song—
    I am the guitar.
I'm the warm, humid night the south wind brings—
    you are the woman walking by the water,
        looking across at the lights.
I am water,
    you are the drinker.
I'm the passerby on the road,
    you are the one who opens her window
        and beckons to me.
You are China,
    I am Mao Zedong's army.
You're a Filipino girl of fourteen,
    I save you
        from an American sailor's clutches.
You're a mountain village
    in Anatolia,
you're my city,
    most beautiful and most unhappy.
You're a cry for help—I mean, you're my country;
    the footsteps running toward you are mine.

1951

LAST WILL AND TESTAMENT

Comrades, if I don't live to see the day
—I mean, if I die before freedom comes—
take me away
and bury me in a village cemetery in Anatolia.

The worker Osman whom Hassan Bey ordered shot
can lie on one side of me, and on the other side
the martyr Aysha, who gave birth in the rye
and died inside of forty days.

Tractors and songs can pass below the cemetery—
in the dawn light, new people, the smell of burnt gasoline,
fields held in common, water in the canals,
no drought or fear of the police.

Of course, we won't hear those songs:
the dead lie stretched out underground
and rot like black branches,
deaf, dumb, and blind under the earth.

But I sang those songs
before they were written,
I smelled the burnt gasoline
before the blueprints for the tractors were drawn.

As for my neighbors,
the worker Osman and the martyr Aysha,
they felt the great longing while alive,
maybe without even knowing it.

Comrades, if I die before that day, I mean
—and it's looking more and more likely—
bury me in a village cemetery in Anatolia,
and if there's one handy,
           a plane tree could stand at my head,
           I wouldn't need a stone or anything.

27 April 1953
Moscow, Barviha Hospital

TO LYDIA IVANNA

How many times we've written poems together,
how many times I've rested my tired head
                in its smoke-blue hands.
I don't think it will hurt me.
But out of respect for your science
        and to make you happy, Lydia Ivanna,
        okay—I'll give up tobacco,
                my prison comrade.
Okay, Lydia Ivanna, I won't get drunk:
no wine, no raki, no vodka,
                not even on New Year's Eve
                or holidays
                        or even on Kostya's birthday.
Yes, that's the easiest:
I don't care if I never touch the stuff.
Okay, I'll put my sick heart to bed
at the stroke of ten
with the birds and children.
And yet, late at night
                in winter especially, how I love
to cross Red Square
quietly, without disturbing
                the big man's sleep,
and walk the banks
        of the Moscow River
or, Lydia Ivanna, to sit up till dawn
        in the light of a master's book.
Okay, I'll abstain for at least six months
from my lover's lips.
We're apart anyway.

I know, comrade Lydia Ivanna,
it's imperative I follow your orders—

or else a third coronary,
my heart exploding like a hand grenade.
I know.
But you say joy,
        anger,
               and grief
are even worse than tobacco,
worse than no sleep.
Yes, but my dear doctor,
how can I keep from bursting with joy
when, say,
        I hear we got the most votes
             in the French elections?
My smart doctor, have a heart:
how can I help getting angry when I think of my country
fighting for its life under the heel of a gang of thugs?
Or look:
        I may never again see
        my Memet and his mother—
my bright-eyed doctor,
          what can I do
             but grieve?
In short,
Lydia Ivanna, don't get mad at me
    if your loving labors come to nothing:
I can't promise to be
    calm, dignified,
        and indifferent,
        like a rock by the sea. . .
If my heart's going to break,
        let it break from anger,
           grief,
             or joy.

29 April 1953
Moscow, Barviha Hospital

THE MAILMAN

from Hungarian travel notes

Whether at dawn or in the middle of the night,
I've carried people news
—of other people, the world, and my country,
    of trees, the birds and the beasts—
        in the bag of my heart.
I've been a poet,
    which is a kind of mailman.
As a child, I wanted to be a mailman,
not via poetry or anything
but literally—a real mail carrier.
In geography books and Jules Verne's novels
my colored pencils drew a thousand different pictures
    of the same mailman—Nazim.
Here, I'm driving a dogsled
    over ice,
canned goods and mail packets
    glint in the Arctic twilight:
I'm crossing the Bering Strait.
Or here, under the shadow of heavy clouds on the steppe,
I'm handing out mail to soldiers and drinking kefir.
Or here, on the humming asphalt of a big city,
I bring only good news
    and hope.
Or I'm in the desert, under the stars,
a little girl lies burning up with fever,
and there's a knock on the door at midnight:
"Mailman!"
The little girl opens her big blue eyes:
her father will come home from prison tomorrow.
I was the one who found that house in the snowstorm
and gave the neighbor girl the telegram.
As a child, I wanted to be a mailman.

But it's a difficult art in my Turkey.
In that beautiful country
        a mailman bears all manner of pain in telegrams
                and line on line of grief in letters.
As a child, I wanted to be a mailman.
I got my wish in Hungary at fifty.
Spring is in my bag,
letters full of the Danube's shimmer,
                        the twitter of birds,
and the smell of fresh grass—
letters from the children of Budapest
        to children in Moscow.
Heaven is in my bag . . .
One envelope
writes:
"Memet,
Nazim Hikmet's son,
                Turkey."
Back in Moscow I'll deliver the letters
to their addresses one by one.
Only Memet's letter I can't deliver
or even send.
Nazim's son,
highwaymen block the roads—
                your letter can't get through.

May 1954

MESSAGE

My fellow
        patients,
                you'll get well.
The aches and pains will cease.
Ease will come
        softly, like a warm summer evening
        descending from heavy green branches.

My fellow patients,
hold on a bit longer, hang on.
What waits outside the door is not death
                    but life.
Outside the door
             is the whole bustling world.
You will rise from your beds
             and walk.
You will discover all over again
the taste of salt, bread, and the sun.

To turn yellow as a lemon, melt like a candle,
or collapse suddenly like a rotted sycamore—
my fellow patients,
we're not lemons, candles, or sycamores;
we're people, thank goodness.
We know how to mix hope with our medicine—
how to put our feet down,
             stand our ground,
                and say,
                    "We must live!"

My fellow
        patients,
                we'll get well.

The aches and pains will cease.
Ease will come
      softly,
      like a warm summer evening
      descending from heavy green branches.

30 June 1954
Frantishkovy-Lazny

ABOUT THE SEA

Leaving a jumble of jagged mountains in the west,
our train descended to the warm, humid plain.
A pickup sweated past us on our right,
the driver a dark plump woman in a green dress.
A sailor sat on the burlap sacks in the back,
his cap ribbon flailed in the wind.
A silvery factory with bridges, towers, chimneys, and smoke
passed on our left
like a warship returning to port.

First came its coolness,
and the sharp smell of iodine
mingled with the scent of the apples on the racks.
Then I saw it reflected in the sky:
the air got bluer and bluer.
Then suddenly we were face to face.
It was inside a breakwater,
squeezed between the ships and the docks.
I remembered an eagle at the zoo—
wings drooping at his sides,
sullen head on his chest.

The train entered the station, it disappeared.
The train left the station, again we were suddenly face to face:
the sun rose,
and the cold, steely glare
that studied us through slit-eyes
softened and warmed up at our approach.
I didn't gaze at it and think:
Life bubbles up and dies down like the foam
on this unbounded, endless motion.
I wanted to jump off the car
and run to it, breathless.

Whether in moonlight or broad daylight,
whether it's frothing or flat as a sheet,
to stand on the shore and watch it
kills me.
I feel the sadness
of an empty augur shell.
I must be at the center of its eye—
with fishermen, say, at the nets.
Or, my hand on the tiller,
                              sailing
                                   with my lover.
Or at the captain's side in a storm
or swimming against the current.
I must be in the eye of it.

I thought of Engels.
How beautiful to have your ashes scattered at sea!
But me, I want to be laid in a pine box
and buried on the Anatolian plateau.
At cherry-blossom time
sailors from many different ships
can come and visit our plateau.
And they can sing the same great song
of many different seas.

1954
Tbilisi-Moscow

LAST LETTER TO MY SON

For one thing, hangmen separated us;
for another, this rotten heart of mine
                    played a trick on me.
It isn't in the cards
            that I'll see you again.

I know
as a young man you'll be like a sheaf of wheat
    —tall, blond, and lean,
        like me in my youth—
with your mother's big eyes,
and now and then you'll grow strangely quiet,
your forehead full of light.
You'll probably even have a good voice
                    —mine was awful—
and you'll sing bittersweet, heartbreaking songs . . .
And you'll know how to talk
—I did okay at that myself,
                    when I wasn't too upset—
words will be honey on your tongue.
Yes, Memet,
                you'll drive the girls crazy . . .
It's hard
    to bring up a boy without a father.
Go easy on your mother, son—
            I couldn't make her happy,
                        but you try.

Your mother is
    as strong and soft as silk;
she'll be as beautiful
    when she's a grandmother
        as she was the day I first saw her

on the Bosporus
at seventeen—
she is moonlight and sunshine, a heart cherry,
a true beauty.

Your mother
and I said good-bye one morning,
thinking we'd meet again,
but we couldn't.
She is the kindest
and smartest of mothers—
may she live to be a hundred!

I don't fear death.
Still,
it's no fun
to startle in the middle of work sometimes
or count the days
before falling asleep alone.
You can never have enough of the world,
Memet, never enough . . .

Don't live in the world as if you were renting
or here only for the summer,
but act as if it was your father's house . . .
Believe in seeds, earth, and the sea,
but people above all.
Love clouds, machines, and books,
but people above all.
Grieve
for the withering branch,
the dying star,
and the hurt animal,
but feel for people above all.
Rejoice in all the earth's blessings—

darkness and light,
the four seasons,
but people above all.

Memet,
our Turkey
     is one sweet
          country.
And its people,
     its real people,
          are hard-working, serious, and brave
               but frightfully poor.
Its people are long-suffering.
But it will turn out good.
You and your people there
will build communism—
you'll see it with your eyes and touch it with your hands.

Memet,
I'll die far from my language and my songs,
my salt and bread,
homesick for you and your mother,
my friends and my people,
but not in exile,
     not in some foreign land—
I will die in the country of my dreams,
     in the white city of my best days.

Memet,
     my son,
     I leave you in the care
          of the Turkish Communist Party.

I go
  at peace.
The life that's coming to an end in me

will survive for a time in you
    but will last forever in our people.

1955
Moscow

LETTER FROM ISTANBUL

My dear,
I'm so tired
I'm writing lying down.
I saw my face in the mirror—I look green.
It's freezing out: summer will never come.
We need thirty liras of wood each week—
                              not easy to manage.
A while ago, when I was working at the table,
I had to put a blanket over me.
The windows are broken, frames and all,
the doors won't close—
we can't possibly live here anymore,
                              we'll have to move,
or the house will come crashing down on us.
But rents are sky-high . . .
Why am I telling you all this?
You'll worry,
but who else can I tell my troubles to?
I'm sorry.

If it would just warm up, really warm up,
                              especially nights.
I'm sick and tired of being cold.
I go to Africa in my dreams.
Once I was in Algiers.
It was hot.
A bullet pierced my forehead.
All my blood gushed out,
                              but I didn't die . . .
Something has come over me:
I suddenly feel ancient
—yet you know
                    I'm not even forty—
I feel as if I'm very old.

I say it, too,
and when I do, they get mad—
                    everybody lectures me.
Anyway, let's drop it . . .

They made a movie of Chekhov's *La Cigale*.
It was shown in Paris. Everyone loved it.
Is it all that poor, silly woman's fault?
I both like the doctor
                    and can't forgive the bastard.
In the end, who's more unhappy?
                    Who, and because of whom?

The radio played some Paraguayan folk songs.
They were written on rough leaves
with love, the sun, and human sweat,
bitter and hopeful at once.
I liked them.

A letter came from Adviyé—
she says she misses me so much,
says she can't forget me.
I was stunned.
In all the years
since you left the country,
she neither knocked on my door
                    nor so much as sent word.
We even met on the street
one holiday morning—
she turned her head and walked right by.
We were such close friends.
But friendship's like a tree:
once it dries up,
                    it won't bloom again.
I didn't answer her—
what good would it do?

Even if she stops by my house now,
I'll have nothing to say to her.
I have nothing against her, either.
Let her live happily ever after.
I hear she found a rich husband—
the man's a sickly thing
                  and a maniac, too,
yet Adviyé was such a lively woman . . .

I just checked our son:
he's sound asleep, rosy and blond.
His blanket was off; I covered him up.
The radio also gave some bad news tonight:
Irène Joliot-Curie died.
She was still young.
Years ago
I read a book
about her mother.
In one place it mentioned two daughters,
I can still see the lines—
Like two blond Greek statues, it said.
And now one of those kids is dead.
How can I say this?
A great scientist, a great woman,
she's also that blond little girl
now dead of leukemia.
Her death shook me—
I cried tonight
                for Irène Joliot-Curie.
If they'd said,
          Irène, how strange,
              Irène, if they'd said,
                  when you're dead,
a woman in Istanbul,
someone you don't know at all,
will cry for you—

if they'd said—
she'd have laughed.
I thought of her husband.
If I wrote a letter
and sent him my condolences,
I thought.
But I don't know his address.
If I'd said, *Paris. Frédéric Joliot*—
would it have gone?

I read in the paper
a French writer also died.
I'm sure you've never heard of him.
Anyway, he was very old
and an egotist on top of it—
a sneaky,
nasty number.
He spent his whole life mocking everything:
he didn't love anyone or anything
but cats and dogs,
and then only his own.
He gave an interview a couple days before he died—
he thinks he's mocking death,
but you can tell he's very scared.
I saw a picture of him, too:
make my grandmother a man
and put a skullcap on his head,
and there you'd have him.
A skinny old guy
totally alone.
I felt sorry for him, too,
maybe because he looked like my grandmother
or maybe because of his loneliness . . .
I pitied him,
but it's not the same.
I grieve for Irène Curie,

I think of her husband and kids,
but, what's more, I feel sorry for the world,
                because a great woman is dead.

Here's some good news—
your lazy son is learning how to read.
The rascal has made great progress:
hold, run, book, pen, bag . . .
Not bad, eh?
He likens each letter to something:
A is a house,
        B a fat man,
                T a hammer.
I'm so scared he'll turn out lazy.
I'm always trying to find work for him.
If he was a girl, it would be easy.
A woman can do any kind of work at any age.
But a five-year-old boy—
                    what can he do?

Ah, if it would just get warm . . .
It *must!*
My letter has gone on and on.
Take good care of yourself,
write me right away,
don't forget me.
Write me right away.
Don't kid yourself and say,
Munevver's smart—
whatever happens, she'll manage, and so on.
I'm lost without you.
Don't forget me.
Take good care of yourself.
I kiss your eyes, my dear.
Good night.

Take good care of yourself.
Write me right away.
Don't worry yourself about my troubles,
                    forget them.
                    Don't forget me . . .

1956

175

IN THE SNOWY NIGHT WOODS

The beeches deep in snow,
I walk the dark woods
In sorrow, sorrow.
Your hand, where is your hand?

The snow the color of moonlight,
My boots heavy in the night,
The song that's sung in me
Is calling me, but where?

Is my country the farthest
Away, or my youth or the stars?
A window in the beech forest
Glows yellow-warm.

What if, as I pass by,
Someone calls me to come in
And I come in and bow deeply,
Greeting those inside the house.

The old calendar says
Spring came in today.
The toys I sent my Memet
Were all returned to me.

His pickup sits brooding, hurt
Its spring never got wound up,
And Memet never got to sail
His white boat in the tub.

The snow is fluffy, clean.
Softly I walk on.
Last night at half-past one
Beirut died—I knew him.

I have a tawny rug of his
And a book, signed.
The book will pass from hand to hand,
The rug will last another hundred years.

I left my budding rose
In my city of seven hills.
There is no shame in dreading death
Or thoughts of dying.

The strangest of our powers
Is the courage to live
Knowing that we will die,
Knowing nothing more true.

Is my country the farthest
Away, or my youth or the stars?
Tell me, Bayramoghlu,
Is there a village on the other side of death?

At night, the beeches deep
In snow, I walk the forest.
All around me I see clear
As day in the darkness.

If I turned off right now—
The path, train tracks, the valley—
From fifteen miles away
Moscow would be a bright glow.

14 March 1956
Peredelkino

NEW YEAR'S EVE

The snow falling hard through the night
sparkled in the starlight.
There is a house on a street in a city,
a wooden house so far away.

The child sleeping on the pillow
is plump and blond—my son.
There are no guests, no one.
Poor Istanbul out the window.

Shrill whistles screamed outside.
Loneliness feels like prison.
Munevver closed her book
and softly cried.

There is a house on a street in a city,
a wooden house so far away.
The snow falling hard through the night
sparkled in the starlight.

23 March 1956
Peredelkino

ELEGY FOR SATAN

My dog's name was Satan.
"Was" has nothing to do with his name—
nothing happened to his name.
And he wasn't anything like his name.
Devils are cruel:
the cruel are sly and lie,
but they aren't smart.
My dog was smart.

I helped to kill my dog a little, too:
I didn't know how to take care of him.
If you can't care for it,
         don't even plant a tree.
A tree that dries up in your hands
         becomes a curse.
"A person learns to swim in water," you say.
True.
But if you drown,
         you drown alone.

Mornings now I wake up
and listen—
no one scratching at my door.
I feel like crying.
I'm ashamed I can't cry.
He was like a person.
Most animals are like people—
         and like good people, too.
Under the command of friendship, his thick neck was hair-thin.
His freedom was in his teeth and legs,
         his politesse in his long bushy tail.

We used to miss each other.
He would speak of the gravest matters:
of hunger, of being full, of love.
But he didn't know longing for home.
That's on my head.
When the poet went to heaven,
        he said: "Ah, but my country..."

He died
the way everyone dies,
whether human, animal, or plant—
on a bed or on the ground, in the air or in water,
suddenly, waiting, or asleep—
the way everyone dies,
the way I'm going to die,
the way we're going to die...

Today it's ninety-eight in the shade.
I gaze at the forest from the balcony:
tall slender pines rise deep red
against the steel-blue sky.
The people sweating,
the dogs' tongues hanging out,
they're all headed for the lake to swim.
Leaving their heavy bodies on the shore,
they'll know the happiness of fish.

June 1956
Peredelkino

FAUST'S HOUSE

Below the towers, under the arcades,
I wander through Prague late
                at night.
The sky is an alembic distilling gold in the dark—
an alchemist's still over a deep-blue flame.
I walk down the hill toward Charles Square:
on the corner, next to the clinic there,
          is Doctor Faust's house set back in a garden.

I knock on the door.
The doctor isn't home.
As we all know,
on a night like this
              about two hundred years ago,
the Devil took him
             through a hole in the ceiling.

I knock on the door.
In this house I, too, will hand Satan a deed—
I, too, signed the deed with my blood.
I don't want gold from him
        or knowledge or youth.
I've had it with exile,
        I give up!
If I could have just one hour in Istanbul. . .

I knock and knock on the door.
But the door doesn't open.
Why?
Am I asking the impossible, Mephistopheles?
Or isn't my tattered soul
worth buying?

In Prague the moon is rising lemon-yellow.
I stand outside Doctor Faust's house
at midnight, knocking on the closed door.

22 November 1956

PRAGUE DAWN

In Prague it's growing light
and snowing—
        sleety,
           leaden.
In Prague the baroque slowly lights up:
               uneasy, distant,
        its gilt grief-blackened.
The statues on Charles Bridge
    look like birds descended from a dead star.

In Prague the first trolley has left the garage,
its windows glow yellow and warm.
But I know
        it's ice-cold inside:
no passenger's breath has warmed it.
In Prague Pepik drinks his coffee and milk,
the wood table spotless in the white kitchen.
In Prague it's growing light
and snowing—
        sleety,
          leaden.

In Prague a cart—
        a one-horse wagon—
      passes the Old Jewish Cemetery.
The cart is full of longing for another city,
         I am the driver.
In Prague the baroque slowly lights up:
             uneasy, distant,
       its gilt grief-blackened.
In Prague's Jewish Cemetery, death is breathless, stone-still.
Ah my rose, ah my rose,
exile is worse than death...

20 December 1956

NOON IN PRAGUE

Master Hanus's Clock

It stopped snowing first on the hill,
                up by Prague Castle.
Then, suddenly, a cool blue
                descended on the chestnuts, clear
            and soft.
                      And with a gentle glow.

The poet, far from home
and riddled with longing,
stood all alone
                in the square in Old Town.
High on a Gothic wall,
                Master Hanus's clock
                    struck noon.

In their gilt robes,
St. Peter at the head,
the tired twelve apostles
                emerged from the clock.
And Judas with his purse
and faith, cruelty and evil.
"And we no sooner came than here we're leaving."
And a stone janissary there below
                in his solitary sorrow.
And Death tolling the bells
and, above, a cock crowing.

The poet, far from home
and riddled with longing,
            looked on, elsewhere.
A soft, cool blue
            descended on the square
                    at noon.

29 December 1956

OPTIMISTIC PRAGUE

1957, January 17.
Nine o'clock exactly.
Sun-bright dry cold, no lies,
dry cold rose-pink,
sky-blue dry cold.
My red mustache nearly freezes.
The city of Prague is etched on cut glass
    with a diamond point.
If I touch it, it will ring:
    gold-edged, clear, white.
It's exactly nine o'clock
    on all the towers
        and my watch.
Dry cold sun-bright, rose-pink,
sky-blue dry cold.
It's exactly nine o'clock.
This minute, this second,
    not a single lie was uttered in Prague.
This minute, this second,
    women gave birth without pain,
and not a single hearse
    went down a single street.
This minute
    all the charts climbed
    in favor of the sick.
For a moment
    all the women were beautiful, all the men wise,
    and the manikins weren't sad.
Now
    children answered all the questions in school
    without stammering.
Now
    there was coal in all the stoves,

heat in all the radiators,
and the dome of the Black Tower
    was covered with gold once more.
For a moment
    the blind forgot their darkness,
    the hunchbacks their humps.
For a moment
    I didn't have any enemies,
and no one hoped
    the old days would return.
Now
    Wenceslaus got off his bronze horse
    and mixed with the crowd—
    no one could tell who he was.
For a moment
    you loved me
    like you've never loved anyone. . .
This minute, this second,
    sun-bright dry cold, no lies,
    dry cold rose-pink,
    sky-blue dry cold.
The city of Prague is etched on cut glass
    with a diamond point.
If I touch it, it will ring:
    gold-edged, clear, white.

TO SAMET VURGUN

I finally made it to your city,
but I was late, Samet,
we couldn't get together:
I was late by the space of death.
I didn't want to hear your voice
on tape, Samet—
I can't look at pictures of the dead
                    without totally dying.

But the day will come
when I'll totally separate you from yourself, Samet.
You'll enter the world of respectable memories.
And I'll lay flowers on your grave
            without tears in my eyes.

Then the day will come
            when what happened to you
            will happen to me, too, Samet.

25 February 1957
Baku

188

I GOT A LETTER FROM MUNEVVER SAYING

Nazim, tell me about the city where I was born.
I was still little when I left Sofia,
but they say I knew Bulgarian . . .
What kind of a city is it?
I heard from my mother
Sofia's small,
but it must have grown—
just think,
        it's been forty-one years.
I remember a "Boris Park."
My nanny took me there mornings.
It must be the biggest park in Sofia.
I still have pictures of me taken in it . . .
A park with lots of sun and shade.
Go sit there.
Maybe you'll run across the bench where I played.
But benches don't last forty years;
they'd have rotted and been replaced.
Trees are best—
they outlive memories.
One day, go sit under the oldest chestnut.
Forget everything,
even our separation—
just think of me.

1957

I WROTE A LETTER TO MUNEVVER SAYING

The trees are still standing, the old benches dead and gone.
"Boris Park" is now "Freedom Park."
Under the chestnut I just thought of you
and you alone—I mean Memet,
just you and Memet, I mean my country . . .

1957

FROM SOFIA

I entered Sofia on a spring day, my sweet.
Your native city smelled of linden trees.

It is my fate
to roam the world without you,
what can we do. . .

In Sofia, trees mean more than walls.
Trees and people blend together here,
                especially the poplar
                about to step into my room
                and sit on the red kilim. . .

Is Sofia a big city?
Grand avenues don't make a city big, my rose,
but the poets remembered in its monuments.
                Sofia is a big city. . .

Evenings here people pour out into the streets:
women and children, young and old,
what laughter, such noise and bustle,
            the buzzing crowd up and down,
        side by side, arm in arm, hand in hand. . .

Ramazan nights in Istanbul,
people used to promenade this way
                (that was before your time, Munevver).
No. . . Those nights are gone. . .
If I were in Istanbul now,
                    would I think to miss them?
But far from Istanbul
                I miss everything,
even the visiting room at the Uskudar prison. . .

I entered Sofia on a spring day, my sweet.
Your native city smelled of linden trees.
Your countrymen welcomed me like you'll never know.
Your native city is my brother's house now.
But even in a brother's house, home can't be forgotten.

Exile is not an easy art to master. . .

24 May 1957
Varna

BOR HOTEL

No way you can sleep nights in Varna,
no way you can sleep:
for the wealth of stars
so close and brilliant,
for the rustle of dead waves on the sand,
of salty weeds
with their pearly shells
and pebbles,
for the sound of a motorboat throbbing like a heart at sea,
for the memories filling my room,
coming from Istanbul,
        passing through the Bosporus,
          and filling my room,
some with green eyes,
some in handcuffs
or holding a handkerchief—
the handkerchief smells of lavender.
No way you can sleep in Varna, my love,
in Varna at the Bor Hotel.

2 June 1957

THE BALCONY

In Kurort-Varna, I look from the balcony
        of the Balkan-Tourist:
the road, trees,
        beyond them sand,
beyond that must be sea and sky—
no,
        neither sea nor sky,
beyond the sand is simply light,
        no end of light...
And this smell of roses in the air
burns the nostrils.
I don't see any roses,
but I can tell from the scent
they're all enormous,
        all very red...
The Polish tourists flock down to the beach,
blond, pink, half-naked...
A swallow spins overhead:
black wings, white breast.
He's not in the least like a bee,
but he's like a bee just the same.
Now you see him, now you don't
as he plunges and soars, giddy
        with his own song...
Cucumber soup in a blue bowl.
They brought a cheese pita
—it's as if I'm in Istanbul—
they brought a cheese pita
with sesame seeds, soft and steaming...
This summer day in Varna,
all big talk aside,
even for a very sick, very exiled poet
this happiness to be alive.

3 June 1957

194

THE LAST BUS

Midnight. The last bus.
The conductor cuts me a ticket.
Neither bad news nor a big dinner
          awaits me at home.
For me, absence waits.
I approach it without sadness
          or fear.

The great dark closes in.
Now I can look at the world
          quietly and at peace.
I'm no longer surprised by a friend's treachery,
          a knife concealed in a handshake.
It's useless—the enemy can't provoke me now.
I passed through the forest of idols
          with my axe—
          how easily they all came down.
I put my beliefs to the test once more,
          I'm thankful most of them turned out pure.
I've never been radiant this way,
          never free like this.

The great dark closes in.
Now I can look at the world
          quietly and at peace.
Suddenly the past comes back
when I'm not looking—
          a word
                    a smell
                              a hand gesture.
          The word is friendly,
                    the smell beautiful—
                    the hand is in a hand, my love.

The call of memory no longer makes me sad.
I have no complaints about memories.
In fact, I can't complain about anything,
not even about my heart
      aching nonstop like a big tooth.

The great dark closes in.
Now neither the seer's pride nor the scribe's claptrap.
I pour bowlfuls of light over my head,
I can look at the sun and not be blinded.
And maybe—what a pity—
      the most beautiful lie
            will no longer seduce me.
Words can't make me drunk anymore,
neither mine nor anyone else's.
That's how it goes, my rose.
Death now is awfully close.
The world is more beautiful than ever.
The world was my suit of clothes,
      I've started undressing.
I was at the window of a train,
      now I'm at the station.
I was inside the house,
      now I'm at the door—it's open.
I love the guests twice as much.
And the heat is blonder than ever,
      the snow whiter than ever.

21 July 1957
Prague

THIS THING CALLED PRAGUE

This thing called Prague is a magic mirror.
I look,
and it shows me in my twenties.
I am like leaping.
I'm like thirty-two healthy teeth,
                and the world is a walnut.
But I want nothing for myself, except
to touch the fingers of the girl I love—
        they hold the greatest secret of the world.
My hands break more bread for my friends
                than for myself.
I kiss all the eyes with trachoma
        in the villages of Anatolia.
Somewhere in the world I fall,
        a martyr to the world revolution.
They pass my heart
        on a velvet cushion
                like a Medal of the Red Flag.
The band plays a funeral march.
We bury our dead in the earth
                under a wall
                like fertile seeds.
And on the earth our songs
        aren't Turkish or Russian or English
                        but just songs.
Lenin lies sick in a snowy forest:
brows knitted, he thinks of certain people,
stares into the white darkness,
                and sees the days to come.
I am like leaping.
I'm like thirty-two healthy teeth,
                and the world is a walnut
                        with a steel shell
                                but full of good news.

197

This thing called Prague is a magic mirror.
I look again,
and it shows me on my deathbed.
Arms stretched out at my sides,
sweat beads on my forehead like drops of wax.
The wallpaper is green.
The sooty rooftops of the big city
out the window aren't Istanbul's.
My eyes are still open
—no one's closed them—
and nobody knows yet.
Bend down,
look into my pupils:
you'll see a young woman
waiting alone at a rainy bus stop.
Close my eyes,
        comrade, and leave the room
                                on tiptoe.

1957

SOME MEMORIES

Close to the border in Bohemia,
at the warm springs of Frantishkovy-Lazny,
the sky swells with hot clouds.
In the Turkish bath, light seeps through the steamed-up window,
the smell of moist flesh mingling with the scent of red roses.

Water flows freely here,
curing heart pains and impotence,
and trees branch out as far as you can see.
It seems that if you stepped down hard enough,
a spring would bubble up, rich in sulfur and calcium,
or a thick beech tree rise all green and white.

I went to see the Three Lilies Hotel.
My friend the Czech poet Nezval
tells me old Goethe worked there
          through many a night.
Many a summer dawn
          caressed his neck bent over his writing table.
The year?
Nezval doesn't know exactly.
1805, he says—
          no, 1800
                    or maybe 1808.
But we both remember another date
          to the day
when tanks with white crosses on their backs
          rode past the Three Lilies Hotel:
it shook so hard
          a table fell over upstairs.
I was in prison then
          in Istanbul.
Tanks rode through Warsaw and Paris,

white crosses on their backs.
I was in prison in Chankiri.
Tanks loomed in the snow
        outside Moscow.
I was in prison in Bursa.
I've known a lot of people in my day,
from all walks of life.
They had traveled far different roads—
asphalt, stone, dirt,
rainy, sunny, wide, narrow.
They'd rested under many different trees.
Some worked like wound-up clocks,
        never missing a beat;
some were wool-gatherers;
some were like seeds, full of hope head to toe;
some were gentle, like lullabies
        in all languages;
some were fiery, like red peppers,
some stubborn
        as mules;
some were stingy, some generous;
some were hooked on women, some on tobacco.
The young
        were like kindling just catching fire,
and the old were as old, sober, and wise
        as the earth.
Most didn't know a word of Russian
        beyond *horascho*
                and maybe *tovarisch*.
But in the winter of 1941,
when tanks loomed in the snow outside Moscow,
all of them were ready to spill their blood
for that great white city
        they'd never visited.
They'd seen it only in their dreams,

construction without end—
       scaffolds, cranes, and people like grains of sand.
They'd seen it in their dreams—
a red square
       ringed with gold domes,
at the center a tomb
           with Lenin inside.
They woke up with tears in their eyes,
in agony.
They'd seen this city in their dreams,
a giant
     apple tree
         blossoming pink and white.

For me, it's not just a city of dreams
           and hopes,
not some unattainable city in the clouds,
      forever beyond the dawn horizon
          in summer on the open sea.
I'm as much an old Muscovite
        as a child of Istanbul.
I had my first audience with its people
at a factory in Krasnaya Presya.
I read my poetry.
Heavy hands resting on their knees,
      a kindly patience in their eyes,
they listened to me as if they knew Turkish
for a good forty-five minutes, more or less,
and clapped.
To this day, whenever I start getting a swelled head,
      the sound of that applause
         brings me to my senses.
Pushkin hadn't been relocated yet
and looked the same then as he does now—
bareheaded, a cape

thrown over his shoulders.
He was tall and dark then, too—
a smart, sad, elegant
St. Petersburg gentleman.
Several times a week,
early mornings or late afternoons,
I'd stick one of our big books under my arm,
stuff my cheeks with sunflower seeds,
      and go sit on a bench near him—
      the second on the left.
In winter it smelled of fresh snow;
in summer, cool leaves.
This spot worked miracles:
I'd open my book,
and what I couldn't get in class at the university
          would suddenly be clear . . .
There's a courtyard off the Arbat.
On winter nights
its brick walls glow,
floor on warm floor,
with orange, blue, and gold windows.
A young man from Istanbul
      shivers in the snowy courtyard for hours.
Tamara's shadow comes and goes
      in the blue window on the top floor.
This city is my city.
I came here at nineteen,
      arriving at Kiev Station
          three hours late.
I saw a man in a cloth cap—
      I can still picture him.
He was either in a poster
      on the wall
or on the platform
      under the broken glass.

Either way,
       he stood a head taller
              than other men,
casually leaning on his sledgehammer.
I went up to him,
       took off my fur hat,
            and saluted the city's new lord and master.
The year was 1922.
Ah, those were the days.
My heart leaping like a fish in water,
the gloom gone to my head like wine,
I'd come from Anatolia via Batum
with just one question for Comrade Lenin ...

1957

OPTIMISM

I write poems
they don't get published
but they will

I'm waiting for a letter with good news
maybe it will arrive the day I die
but it will come for sure

the world's not run by governments or money
but people rule
a hundred years from now
maybe
but it will be for sure

2 September 1957
Leipzig

THIRTY YEARS AGO

I passed this way thirty years ago.
Four days and nights by train . . .
Now it's under sixty hours,
eight by plane.
Soon Tupolevs will make
Moscow-Baku
two hours and ten minutes . . .

Thirty years ago
songs filled the train—
songs like a handkerchief waved at a lover,
like a flag leading us on.
The same songs
of my youth
still fill the train.

Thirty years ago
a Komsomol girl rode the train
in a leather jacket and a red scarf,
a book in her calloused hands—
                    Mayakovsky.
Now a Komsomol girl rides the train
in a rayon blouse,
returning from the harvest in Kazakhstan
with a book in her calloused hands—
                    Mayakovsky.

I passed this way thirty years ago.
The train carried heartbroken brides then, too—
White Russians had hanged their men—
but not brides widowed by Fascist bullets.

The soldiers then had memories
of retreating White armies.
But not
        of the flaming streets of Berlin . . .

Thirty years ago
Kharkov was a city,
but it hadn't been leveled to the ground
        and raised ten times higher.
The steppes along the Don looked the same then
—shadeless and flat—
but without tractors from Kharkov.
Rostov was a port,
but it didn't harbor
                waters from the Baltic.
The Caspian
still looks as heavy
        as molten lead,
but now we've planted
        oil trees
        in wells at the bottom of the sea.
The barren place called Sumgait
        with its bone-dry earth
hadn't become a green city
        with factories and a hundred thousand people.
Poetry was found in Azerbaijan,
but not Samet's.
The moon was up there,
but all alone—
no little brother yet.

Thirty years ago
I was here, but my son wasn't.
Maybe he'll pass this way in thirty years,
maybe I won't be here.

For sure "maybe"—is eighty-five too much?
Maybe I won't be here,
but who knows what will be?
I'm very curious what will happen.

I passed this way thirty years ago.

12–13 October 1957
Moscow-Baku

A FABLE OF FABLES

We stand at the source,
the plane tree and I.
Our images reflect
off the river.
The water-dazzle
lights up the plane tree and me.

We stand at the source,
the plane tree, me, and the cat.
Our images reflect
off the river.
The water-dazzle
lights up the plane tree, me, and the cat.

We stand at the source,
the plane tree, me, the cat, and the sun.
Our images reflect
off the river.
The water-dazzle
lights up the plane tree, me, the cat, and the sun.

We stand at the source,
the plane tree, me, the cat, the sun, and our lives.
Our images reflect
off the river.
The water-dazzle
lights up the plane tree, me, the cat, the sun, and our lives.

We stand at the source.
The cat will be the first to go,
its image in the water will dissolve.
Then I will go,
my image in the water will dissolve.
Then the plane tree will go,

its image in the water will dissolve.
Then the river will go,
the sun alone remaining,
and then it, too, will go.

BACH'S CONCERTO NO. 1 IN C MINOR

Fall morning in the vineyard:
    in row after row the repetition of knotty vines,
        of clusters on the vines,
        of grapes in the clusters,
        of light on the grapes.

At night, in the big white house,
    the repetition of windows,
    each lit up separately.

The repetition of all the rain that falls
    on earth, trees, and the sea,
    on my hands, face, and eyes,
    and of the drops crushed on the glass.

The repetition of my days
    that are alike,
    my days that are not alike.

The repetition of the thread in the weave,
    the repetition in the starry sky,
    and the repetition of "I love you" in all languages.
    The repetition of the tree in the leaves
    and of the pain of living, which ends in an instant
        on every deathbed.

The repetition in the snow—
    the light snow,
    the heavy wet snow,
    the dry snow,
the repetition in the snow that whirls
in the blizzard and drives me off the road.

The children are running in the courtyard;
in the courtyard the children are running.
An old woman is passing by on the street;
on the street, an old woman is passing by;
passing by on the street is an old woman.

At night, in the big white house,
      the repetition of windows,
      each lit up separately.

In the clusters, of grapes,
on the grapes, of light.

To walk toward the good, the just, the true,
to fight for the good, the just, the true,
to seize the good, the just, the true.
Your silent tears and smile, my rose,
your sobs and bursts of laughter, my rose,
the repetition of your shining white teeth when you laugh.

Fall morning in the vineyard:
      in row after row the repetition of knotty vines,
            of clusters on the vines,
            of grapes in the clusters,
            of light on the grapes,
            of my heart in the light.

My rose, this is the miracle of repetition—
to repeat without repeating.

23 February 1958
Warsaw

CONVERSATION WITH DEAD NEZVAL

Soon after you left
it got cold and snowed.
When that happens, they say the sky
is weeping for the dead.
But that's spring, you know.
On the 13th of April the sun opened up.
Prague suddenly smiled
even there at the cemetery.
Though they still speak of you
almost as if they were praying,
your black-draped photo
stands bright and sunny in the store window.
The weather could turn bad again,
but then we're facing May—
May in Prague, you know,
green, gold-yellow.
When it attacks the streets,
young girls wipe grief clean
like window panes,
and the grief you left us
will vanish like your shadow
from the sidewalks of Prague.
This world. . . But to tell the truth,
the life-loving, smart,
good-hearted dead
don't want forty days of mourning
or say, "After me the deluge!"
Leaving behind some helpful things
—a few words, a tree, a smile—
each gets up and goes
and does not burden the living
with the darkness of the tomb,
carrying the weight

of his stone all alone.
And because they ask nothing
from the living,
it's as if they aren't dead. . .
Nezval, I know
you're like that, too—
you, too, are one of the good-hearted,
world-loving, smart
dead of Prague.

20 April 1958
Prague

ELEGY FOR MIKHAIL REFILI

This is the leaf fall of my generation,
most of us won't make winter.

I went crazy, Refili,
when I got the news. . .
What was I saying. . .
          Do you remember, Mikhail. . .
But you don't have any memory now,
you don't have a nose, mouth, or eyes. . .
Brother, you're a pile of bones
         in a Baku cemetery.
What was I saying. . .
One New Year's Eve in Moscow,
below the decked-out pine tree on our table,
you glowed like a big toy.
Your bright eyes, bald head,
         respectable belly.
Outside, a snowy forest plunged in darkness.
I looked at you and thought:
    His excellency—pleased as an old barrel of wine,
    hardy as an old wine barrel.
    He'll long outlive me.
    And after I'm gone he'll turn out an article
        or a poem:
    "I met Nazim in Moscow in 1924. . ."
Really, Mikhail, you could have been a poet,
    you were a professor.
But that's not the point.
The best of the work we do, or the worst,
    lives after us.
Yours was middling, I think.
Mine, too.
    I mean, we don't have the consolation our voices

won't be lost in this world.
For my part, I don't mind.
I've succeeded in living without consolation,
and I'll succeed in dying without it—
                        like you, Refili.

5 June 1958
Prague

EARLY FALL

This year, early fall in the deep south,
I steep myself in the sea, sand, and sun,
in trees
and apples as if in honey.
At night the air smells like harvested wheat—
the night sky meets the dusty road,
and I blend with the stars.

My rose,
    I've gotten so close
        to the sea, sand, sun, apples, stars.
Now it's time I got lost
      in the sea, sand, sun, apples, stars.

8 September 1958
Arhipo Osipovka

THE BEES

The bees, like big drops of honey
carrying grapevines to the sun,
came flying out of my youth;
the apples, these heavy apples,
          are also from my youth;
the gold-dust road,
these white pebbles in the stream,
my faith in songs,
my freedom from envy,
the cloudless day, this blue day,
the sea flat on its back, naked and warm,
my longing, these bright teeth and full lips—
they all came to this Caucasian village
like big drops of honey on the legs of bees
out of my youth, the youth I left somewhere
                before I was through.

13 September 1958
Arhipo Osipovka

WINDOWS

I don't know if it was early morning
late afternoon
or maybe midnight
I don't know
windows entered my room
with curtains and without
I like print curtains
but there were lace curtains too
and black shades
I ran them up and down
till some wouldn't come down
and others wouldn't spring back up
and windows with broken glass
              I cut my hand
some had no glass
windows without glass sadden me
like empty eyeglass frames

windows
rain lashed your glass
its long hair red and grieving
a cigarette hanging from my lips
I was singing a song in my head
I like the sound of rain more than my voice

windows
a sea filled your sunny vacancy on the fifth floor
a blue-sapphire sea
I quietly slipped it on my little finger
and kissed it three times with tears in my eyes
kissed and put it to my forehead three times

windows
I got up from the red canopy bed
and pressed my child's nose against your steamed-up glass
the hot room smelled of my young mother
I had measles

windows
I don't know if it was early morning
or maybe midnight
I don't know
stars entered my room
beating against your glass
                    like moths
trying not to touch them
            I opened you windows
            and let the stars out into the night
            the bright endless free night
            the night satellites crossed
wolves stand under the moon
            hungry and sick
wolves stand outside my window
even if I draw the velvet curtains tight
I know they're out there
watching me

windows
I fell out a window
ogling a beauty
everyone laughed at me
the beauty didn't even turn around
maybe she never noticed

windows
windows
the windows of many houses fill my room
I sat in one
and dangled my feet in the clouds
you could almost say
                I was happy

22 September 1958
Pitsunda

THE OLD MAN ON THE SHORE

deep mountains lined up in rows
the pine forest reached to the sea
on the shore an old man lay
stretched out on the pebble beach

and this sun-ripe September day
the distant news of sunken ships
the cool blue of the northeast breeze
caressed the old man's face

his hands were folded on his chest
stubborn and tired like two crabs
the tough hard-shelled triumph
of a journey outlasting time

his salt-wrinkled eyelids
were softly closed
and in the gold-speckled darkness
the old man listened to the roar

the sea the sharp-toothed fish
the flaming dawn
the rocks blooming at the bottom
the nets and the fisherman's home

or maybe the roar came from high
in the pines near the clouds
he knew it would make him dizzy
to look up at them from below

deep mountains lined up in rows
the pine forest reached to the sea
on the shore an old man lay
stretched out on the pebble beach

24 September 1958
Pitsunda

THE OPTIMIST

as a kid he didn't pluck the wings off flies
tie tin cans to cats' tails
lock beetles in matchboxes
or stomp anthills
he grew up
and all those things were done to him
I sat at his deathbed
he said to read him a poem
about the sun and the sea
nuclear reactors and satellites
the greatness of humanity

8 September 1958
Baku

BECAUSE

They'll go to the moon
                and beyond,
to places even telescopes can't see.
But when will no one go hungry
                                on earth
            or fear others
            or push them around,
            shun them
            or steal their hope?
Because I responded to this question
                I'm called a Communist.

THIS JOURNEY

We open doors,
close doors,
pass through doors,
and reach at the end of our only journey
                    no city,
                    no harbor—
the train derails,
the ship sinks
the plane crashes.
The map is drawn on ice.
But if I could
        begin this journey all over again,
                            I would.

1958
Leningrad

THE ICEBREAKER

The icebreaker leads the way;
our boat shudders in its wake.
I watch from my cabin porthole:
the sea is frozen solid white.
I come from Istanbul—
I grew up by the warm, salt sea.
We like our colors, light, and life clear-cut.
We have poppy fields,
streets,
covered bazaars,
and pigeons,
but the liveliest thing of all is our sea.
Our sea is blue-green,
more restless than a northeaster
       and quicker than dolphins.
Where I come from, summer noons
      when not a leaf is moving,
       it alone still moves,
         endlessly
           trembling.
We never lose its scent.
I watch from my cabin porthole:
the sea is frozen
       solid
         white.
I watch,
    devastated.

1959
Leningrad-Stockholm

TWO LOVES

Two loves can't exist in one heart.
What a lie—
it happens all the time.

Tonight in this cold, rainy city
I'm stretched out on my back in my hotel,
staring at the ceiling.
Clouds cross it
slowly, like trucks passing on the wet asphalt,
and far off to the right
        a gold needle shines at the top
                of a white building
maybe a hundred stories tall.
Clouds cross the ceiling
filled with the sun, like watermelon boats.
I'm sitting in a bay window,
the light off the water hitting my face—
a river or the sea?

What's on that tray
with the roses—
wild strawberries or black mulberries?
Am I in a field of jonquils
or a snowy beech grove?
The women I love laugh and cry
                in two languages.
Friends, what brought you together?
You don't know each other.
Where do you wait for me—
at the Sycamore Café in Beyazit or in Gorki Park?
Tonight in this cold, rainy city
I'm stretched out on my back in my hotel.
My eyes burn, wide-open.

I hear a tune
harmonicas started end with a lute.
My longings for two distant cities
get all tangled up inside me.

To jump out of bed
and run through the rain
to the station:
"Drive, engineer—

                brother, take me there!"
"Where?"

17 July 1959

WAITRESS

One of the waitresses
        at Berlin's Astoria Restaurant
       was a jewel of a girl.
She'd smile at me across her heavy trays.
She looked like the girls of the country I've lost.
Sometimes she had dark circles under her eyes—
         I don't know why.
I never got to sit
     at one of her tables.

He never once sat at one of my tables.
He was an old man.
And he must have been sick—
        he was on a special diet.
He could gaze at my face so sadly,
        but he couldn't speak German.
For three months he came in for three meals a day,
then he disappeared.
Maybe he went back to his country,
       maybe he died before he could.

23 July 1959

TO VERA

A tree grows inside me—
I brought it as a seedling from the sun.
Its leaves quiver like fish, like flames,
and its fruits sing like birds.

Spacemen have already landed
on the star inside me.
They speak the language I heard in my dream:
no bossing, boasting, or whining.

A white road runs through me,
open to ants carrying grains of wheat
and trucks of merrymakers screaming past
but closed to all hearses.

Inside me, time stands still
like the sweetest red rose.
That it's Friday, tomorrow's Saturday,
or the end's in sight—I couldn't care less.

15 January 1960
Kislovodsk

EARLY LIGHT

The telegraph poles in the early light,
                              the road.
The dresser mirror brightening,
                    the table,
                                        slippers.
Things make out one another once again.
In our room the early light unfolds like a sail,
the cool air diamond-blue.
The stars pale—
far off, pebbles bleach white
              deep in the river of the sky.
My rose sleeps,
         her head on the enormous feather pillow.
Her hands on the quilt look like two white tulips.
Birds start singing in her hair.
The city in the early light:
the trees are wet, the smokestacks hot.
The first footsteps caressing the asphalt
         pass through our room,
                 the hum of the first engine,
                       the first laugh,
                       the first curse.
The steamed-up glass case of the pastry cart,
the driver in boots entering the dairy store,
the neighbors' crying kid,
the dove in the blue poster,
the manikin with yellow shoes
               in the window,
and Chinese fans of sandalwood
and her full red lips
and the happiest and freshest of awakenings
         all pass through our room in the early light.
I turn on the radio:

metals with giant names mix with giant numbers,
oil wells race with cornfields.
The shepherd who got the Lenin Medal
      (I saw his picture on the front page,
           his thick mustache black and drooping)
speaks shyly like a young girl.
Then the news from around the world.
Then, as Sputnik III
      circles the earth for the 8878th time
        at six this morning,
my rose opens her big eyes on the pillow.
They're still like smoky mountain lakes:
blue fish flicker in them,
green pines rise in their depths.
They look out deep and flat.
The last of her dreams flashes in the early morning.
I'm illuminated,
I know myself once more.
I'm recklessly happy
      and a bit embarrassed,
        but just a little bit.
In the early morning the light in our room
      is like a sail
        spread for a voyage.
My rose gets out of bed naked like an apricot.
In the early light the bed is snow-white
      like the dove in the blue poster.

February 1960
Kislovodsk

BAKU AT NIGHT

Reaching down to the starless heavy sea
in the pitch-black night,
Baku is a sunny wheatfield.
High above on a hill,
grains of light hit my face by the handfuls,
and the music in the air flows like the Bosporus.
High above on a hill,
my heart goes out like a raft
                        into the endless absence,
                        beyond memory
                        down to the starless heavy sea
                        in the pitch dark.

February 1960

THE CUCUMBER

to Ekber Babayev

The snow is knee-deep in the courtyard
and still coming down hard:
it hasn't let up all morning.
We're in the kitchen.
On the table, on the oilcloth, spring—
on the table there's a very tender young cucumber,
                              pebbly and fresh as a daisy.
We sit around the table staring at it.
It softly lights up our faces
and the very air smells fresh.
We sit around the table staring at it
—amazed,
              thoughtful,
                              optimistic—
as if in a dream.
On the table, on the oilcloth, hope—
on the table, beautiful days,
a cloud seeded with a green sun,
an emerald crowd impatient and on its way,
loves blooming openly—
on the table, there on the oilcloth, a very tender young
                                                cucumber,
                              pebbly and fresh as a daisy.
The snow is knee-deep in the courtyard
and coming down hard.
It hasn't let up all morning.

March 1960
Moscow

MY WOMAN

My woman came with me as far as Brest,
she got off the train and stayed on the platform,
she grew smaller and smaller,
she became a kernel of wheat in the infinite blue,
then all I could see were the tracks.

Then she called out from Poland, but I couldn't answer,
I couldn't ask, "Where are you, my rose, where are you?"
"Come," she said, but I couldn't reach her,
the train was going like it would never stop,
I was choking with grief.

Then patches of snow were rotting on sandy earth,
and suddenly I knew my woman was watching:
"Did you forget me," she asked, "did you forget me?"
Spring marched with muddy bare feet on the sky.

Then stars lighted on the telegraph wires,
darkness lashed the train like rain,
my woman stood under the telegraph poles,
her heart pounding as if she were in my arms,
the poles kept disappearing, she didn't move,
the train was going like it would never stop,
I was choking with grief.

Then suddenly I knew I'd been on that train for years
—I'm still amazed at how or why I knew it—
and always singing the same great song of hope,
I'm forever leaving the cities and women I love,
and carrying my losses like wounds opening inside me,
I'm getting closer, closer to somewhere.

March 1960
Mediterranean Sea

235

VERA WAKING

the chairs are asleep on their feet
                    the same as the table
the rug lies stretched out on its back
                    clutching its design
the mirror is sleeping
the eyes of the windows are closed tight
the balcony sleeps with its legs dangling over the edge
on the opposite roof the chimneys are sleeping
                    the same as the acacias on the sidewalk
the cloud sleeps
          with a star on its chest
the light is asleep indoors and out
you woke up my rose
the chairs awoke
      and scrambled from corner to corner
                    the same as the table
the rug sat up straight
            slowly unfolding its colors
like a lake at sunrise the mirror awakened
the windows opened their big blue eyes
the balcony woke up
          and pulled its legs out of the air
on the opposite roof the chimneys smoked
the acacias on the sidewalk broke into song
the cloud woke up
          and tossed the star on its chest into our room
the light woke up indoors and out
                    flooding your hair
                        it slipped through your fingers
      and embraced your naked waist those white feet of yours

May 1960
Moscow

SEPARATION

separation swings through the air like a steel bar
it keeps smacking me in the face
I'm staggering

I run away it chases me
there's no escaping it
my knees fail I'm falling

separation isn't time or distance
it's the bridge between us
finer than silk thread sharper than a sword

finer than silk thread sharper than a sword
separation is the bridge between us
even when we sit knee to knee

6 June 1960
Berlin-Moscow plane

LOVING YOU

Loving you is like eating bread dipped in salt,
like waking feverish at night
               and putting my mouth to the water faucet,
like opening a heavy unlabeled parcel
               eagerly, happily, cautiously.
Loving you is like flying over the sea
for the first time, like feeling dusk settle
               softly over Istanbul.
Loving you is like saying "I'm alive."

27 August 1960

BECAUSE OF YOU

Because of you, each day is a melon slice
               smelling sweetly of earth.
Because of you, all fruits reach out to me
               as if I were the sun.
Thanks to you, I live on the honey of hope.
You are the reason my heart beats.
Because of you, even my loneliest nights
         smile like an Anatolian kilim on your wall.
Should my journey end before I reach my city,
        I've rested in a rose garden thanks to you.
Because of you I don't let death enter,
        clothed in the softest garments
and knocking on my door with songs
        calling me to the greatest peace.

29 August 1960

SUDDENLY

Suddenly something snaps in me and catches in my throat,
suddenly, in the middle of work, I jump up,
suddenly, in a hotel, in the hall, standing up, I fall into a dream,
suddenly, on the sidewalk, a branch whacks me in the forehead,
suddenly a wolf howls at the moon, miserable, enraged, starved,
suddenly stars hang from a swing in a garden,
suddenly I see myself in the grave,
suddenly my head is a sunny haze,
suddenly I cling to the day I started out as if it wouldn't end,
and every time you float up to the surface . . .

8 September 1960

SIX O'CLOCK

Morning, six o'clock.
I opened the door of the day and stepped in—
a taste of young blue greeted me in the window,
the lines on my forehead remained in the mirror from yesterday,
and behind me a woman's voice came softer than peach fuzz
and, on the radio, news from my country,
and now, my greed filling and overflowing,
I'll run from tree to tree in the orchard of the hours,
and the sun will set, my love,
and I hope that beyond the night
the taste of a new blue will await me, I hope.

14 September 1960

ABOUT US

all I wrote about us is lies
not what happened but what I wished would happen
they were my hungers dangling from your out-of-reach branches
my thirsts rising from the well of my dreams
they were pictures I drew on light

all I wrote about us is the truth
your beauty
      I mean a fruit basket or a picnic in a meadow
my missing you
      I mean being the last streetlamp on the last city block
my jealousy
      I mean running blindfolded among night trains
my happiness
      I mean a sun-struck dam-busting river

all I wrote about us is lies
all I wrote about us is the truth

30 September 1960
Leipzig

STRAW-BLOND

*to Vera Tulyakova,
with my deep respect*

I

at dawn the express entered the station unannounced
it was covered with snow
I stood on the platform my coat collar raised
the platform was empty
a sleeper window stopped in front of me
its curtains were parted
a young woman slept in the lower berth in the twilight
her hair straw-blond eyelashes blue
and her full red lips looked spoiled and pouting
I didn't see who was sleeping in the upper berth
unannounced the express slipped out of the station
I don't know where it came from or where it was going
I watched it leave
I was sleeping in the upper berth
                                    in the Bristol Hotel in Warsaw
I hadn't slept so soundly in years
and yet my bed was wooden and narrow
a young woman slept in another bed
her hair straw-blond eyelashes blue
her white neck long and smooth
she hadn't slept so soundly in years
and yet her bed was wooden and narrow
time sped on we were nearing midnight
we hadn't slept so soundly in years
and yet our beds were wooden and narrow
I'm coming down the stairs from the fourth floor
the elevator is out again
inside mirrors I'm coming down the stairs

I could be twenty I could be a hundred
time sped on I was nearing midnight
on the third floor a woman was laughing behind a door
              a sad rose slowly opened in my right hand
I met a Cuban ballerina at the snowy windows on the second floor
she flashed past my forehead like a fresh dark flame
the poet Nicolas Guillen went back to Havana long ago
for years we sat in the hotel lobbies of Europe and Asia
              drinking the loss of our cities drop by drop
two things are forgotten only with death
the face of our mothers and the face of our cities
wood barges swim into the wind early mornings in winter
              like old rowboats that have cut themselves loose
and in the ashes of a brazier
              my big Istanbul wakes up from sleep
two things are forgotten only with death
the doorman saw me off his cloak sinking into the night
I walked into the icy wind and neon
time sped on I was nearing midnight
they came upon me suddenly
it was light as day but no one else saw
a squad of them
they had jackboots pants coats
arms swastikas on their arms
hands automatics in their hands
they had shoulders helmets on their shoulders but no heads
between their shoulders and their helmets nothing
they even had collars and necks but no heads
they were the soldiers whose deaths are not mourned
I walked on
you could see their fear animal fear
I can't say it showed in their eyes
they didn't have heads to have eyes
you could see their fear animal fear
it showed in their boots

can boots show fear
theirs did
in their fear they opened fire
they fired nonstop at all buildings all vehicles all living things
at every sound the least movement
they even fired at a poster of blue fish on Chopin Street
but not so much as a piece of plaster fell or a window broke
and no one but me heard the shots
the dead even an SS squad the dead can't kill
the dead kill by coming back as worms inside the apple
but you could see their fear animal fear
wasn't this city killed before they were
weren't the bones of this city broken one by one and its skin flayed
weren't bookcovers made from its skin soap from its oil rope
    from its hair
but there it was standing before them
like a hot loaf of bread in the icy night wind
time sped on I was nearing midnight
on Belvedere road I thought of the Poles
they dance a heroic mazurka through history
on Belvedere road I thought of the Poles
in this palace they gave me my first and maybe last medal
the master of ceremonies opened the gilded white door
I entered the hall with a young woman
her hair straw-blond eyelashes blue
and no one was there but us two
plus the aquarelles and delicate chairs and sofas like doll furniture
and you became
            a blue-tinted pastel or a porcelain doll
or maybe a spark from my dream landed on my chest
you slept in the lower berth in the twilight
your white neck long and smooth
you hadn't slept so soundly in years
and here in the Caprice Bar in Cracow
time speeds on we're nearing midnight

separation was on the table between the coffee cup and my glass
you put it there
it was the water at the bottom of a stone well
I lean over and see
an old man dimly smiling at a cloud
I call out
the echoes of my voice return without you
separation was in the cigarette package on the table
the waiter with glasses brought it but you ordered it
it was smoke curling in your eyes
it was at the end of your cigarette
and in your hand waiting to say goodbye
separation was on the table where you rested your elbow
it was in what went through your mind
            in what you hid from me and what you didn't
separation was in your calm
            in your trust in me
it was in your great fear
to fall in love with someone out of the blue as if your door burst open
actually you love me and don't know it
separation was in your not knowing
separation was free of gravity weightless I can't say like a feather
    even a feather weighs something separation was weightless
    but it was there
time speeds on midnight approaches
we walked in the shadow of medieval walls reaching the stars
time sped backward
the echoes of our steps returned like scrawny yellow dogs
they ran behind us and in front
the devil roams Jagiellonian University
digging his nails into the stones
he's out to sabotage the astrolabe Copernicus got from the Arabs
and in the market place under the Cloth Arcade
he's with the Catholic students dancing to rock 'n' roll
time speeds on midnight approaches

the red glow of Nowa Huta lights the clouds
there young workers from the villages cast their souls along with iron
burning into new molds
and casting souls is a thousand times harder than casting iron
the trumpeter who tells the hours in the bell tower of St. Mary's
    Church
sounded midnight
his call rose out of the Middle Ages
                    warned the city of the enemy's approach
and was cut off by an arrow through the throat
the herald died at peace
and I thought of the pain
of dying before announcing the enemy's approach
time speeds on midnight recedes
like a ferry landing gone dark
at dawn the express entered the station unannounced
Prague was all rain
it was an inlaid-silver chest at the bottom of a lake
I opened it
inside a young woman slept among glass birds
her hair straw-blond eyelashes blue
she hadn't slept so soundly in years
I closed the chest and put it on the baggage car
unannounced the express slipped out of the station
arms hanging at my sides I watched it leave
Prague was all rain
you aren't here
you're sleeping in the lower berth in the twilight
the upper berth is empty
you aren't here
one of the world's most beautiful cities is empty
like a glove pulled off your hand
it went dark like mirrors that no longer see you
the waters of the Vltava disappear under bridges like lost nights
the streets are all empty

in all the windows the curtains are drawn
the streetcars go by all empty
      they don't even have conductors or drivers
the coffeehouses are empty
      bars and restaurants too
the store windows are empty
      no cloth no crystal no meat no wine
      not a book not a box of candy not a carnation
and in this loneliness enfolding the city like fog an old man try-
    ing to shake off the sadness of age made ten times worse by
    loneliness throws bread to the gulls from Legionnaires Bridge
      dipping each piece in the blood
      of his too-young heart
I want to catch the minutes
the gold dust of their speed stays on my fingers
a woman sleeps in the lower berth in the sleeper
she hasn't slept so soundly in years
her hair straw-blond eyelashes blue
her hands candles in silver candlesticks
I can't see who's sleeping in the upper berth
if anyone is sleeping there it isn't me
maybe the upper berth is empty
maybe Moscow is in the upper berth
fog has settled over Poland
        over Brest too
for two days now planes can't land or take off
but the trains come and go they go through hollowed-out eyes
since Berlin I was alone in the compartment
the next morning I woke to sun on snowy fields
in the dining car I drank a kind of *ayran* called kefir
the waitress recognized me
she'd seen two of my plays in Moscow
a young woman met me at the station
her waist narrower than an ant's
her hair straw-blond eyelashes blue

I took her hand and we walked
we walked in the sun cracking the snow
spring came early that year
those days they flew news to the evening star
Moscow was happy I was happy we were happy
suddenly I lost you in Mayakovsky Square I lost you suddenly no
    not suddenly because I first lost the warmth of your hand in
    mine then the soft weight of your hand in my palm and then
    your hand
and separation had set in long ago at the first touch of our fingers
but I still lost you suddenly
on the sea of asphalt I stopped the cars and looked inside no you
the boulevards all under snow
yours not among the footprints
I know your footprints in boots shoes stockings bare
I asked the guards
didn't you see
if she took off her gloves you couldn't miss her hands
they're like candles in silver candlesticks
the guards answered very politely
we didn't see
a tugboat breasts the current at Seraglio Point in Istanbul
behind it three barges
awk awk the sea gulls go awk awk
I called out to the barges from Red Square I didn't call to the
    tugboat captain because he wouldn't have heard me over the
    roar of his engine besides he was tired and his coat had no
    buttons
I called out to the barges from Red Square
we didn't see
I stood I'm standing in all the lines in all the streets of Moscow
and I'm asking just the women
old women quiet and patient with smiling faces under wool babushkas
young women rosy-cheeked and straight-nosed in green velvet hats
and young girls very clean and firm and elegant too

maybe there are frightful old women weary young women and
    sloppy girls
                but who cares about them
women spot beauty before men do and they don't forget it
didn't you see
her hair straw-blond eyelashes blue
her black coat has a white collar and big pearl buttons
she got it in Prague
we didn't see
I'm racing the minutes now they're ahead now me
when they're ahead I'm scared I'll lose sight
of their disappearing red lights
when I'm ahead their headlights throw my shadow on the road
    my shadow races ahead of me suddenly I'm afraid I'll lose
    sight of my shadow
I go into theaters concerts movies
I didn't try the Bolshoi you don't like tonight's opera
I went into Fisherman's Bar in Istanbul and sat talking sweetly
    with Sait Faik I was out of prison a month his liver was hurt-
    ing and the world was beautiful
I go into restaurants with brassy orchestras famous bands
I ask gold-braided doormen and aloof tip-loving waiters
hatcheck girls and the neighborhood watchman
we didn't see
the clock tower of the Strastnoi Monastery rang midnight
actually both tower and monastery were torn down long ago
they're building the city's biggest movie house there
that's where I met my nineteenth year
we recognized each other right away
yet we hadn't seen each other not even photos
we still recognized each other right away we weren't surprised
    we tried to shake hands
but our hands couldn't touch forty years of time stood between us
a North Sea frozen and endless
and it started snowing in Strastnoi now Pushkin Square

I'm cold especially my hands and feet
yet I have wool socks and fur-lined boots and gloves
he's the one without socks his feet wrapped in rags inside old
    boots his hands bare
the world is the taste of a green apple in his mouth
the feel of a fourteen-year-old girl's breasts in his hands
songs go for miles and miles in his eyes death measures a hand's-span
and he has no idea what all will happen to him
only I know what will happen
because I believed everything he believes
I loved all the women he'll love
I wrote all the poems he'll write
I stayed in all the prisons he'll stay in
I passed through all the cities he will visit
I suffered all his illnesses
I slept all his nights dreamed all his dreams
I lost all that he will lose
her hair straw-blond eyelashes blue
her black coat has a white collar and big pearl buttons
I didn't see

                              II

my nineteenth year crosses Beyazit Square comes out on Red Square
and goes down to Concorde I meet Abidin and we talk squares
the day before yesterday Gagarin circled the biggest square of all
    and returned
Titov too will go around and come back seventeen-and-a-half
    times even but I don't know about it yet
I talk spaces and shapes with Abidin in my attic hotel room
and the Seine flows on both sides of Notre Dame
from my window at night I see the Seine as a sliver of moonlight
    on the wharf of the stars
and a young woman sleeps in my attic room

mixed with the chimneys of the Paris roofs
she hasn't slept so soundly in years
her straw-blond hair curled her blue eyelashes like clouds on her face
with Abidin I discuss the space and shape of the atom's seed
we speak of Rumi whirling in space
Abidin paints the colors of unlimited speed
I eat up the colors like fruit
and Matisse is a fruitpeddler he sells the fruits of the cosmos
like our Abidin and Avni and Levni
and the spaces shapes and colors seen by microscopes and rocket
    portholes
and their poets painters and musicians
in the space of one-fifty by sixty Abidin paints the surge forward
    the way I can see and catch fish in water that's how I see and
    catch the bright moments flowing on Abidin's canvas
and the Seine is like a sliver of moonlight
a young woman sleeps in a sliver of moonlight
how many times have I lost her how many times have I found
    her and how many more times will I lose her and find her
that's the way it is girl that's how it is I dropped part of my life
    into the Seine from St. Michel Bridge
one morning in drizzling light that part will catch Monsieur Dupont's
    fishline
Monsieur Dupont will pull it out of the water along with the blue
    picture of Paris he won't make anything of my life it won't be
    like a fish or a shoe
Monsieur Dupont will throw it back along with the blue picture of Paris
the picture will stay where it was
the part of my life will flow with the Seine into the great cemetery
    of rivers
I woke to the rustle of blood in my veins
my fingers weightless
my fingers and toes about to snap off take to the air and circle
    lazily overhead
no right and left or up and down

I should ask Abidin to paint the student shot in Beyazit Square
and comrade Gagarin and comrade Titov whose name fame
or face I don't know yet and those to come after him and the
young woman asleep in the attic
I got back from Cuba this morning
in the space that is Cuba six million people whites blacks yellows
mulattoes are planting a bright seed the seed of seeds joyously
can you paint happiness Abidin
but without taking the easy way out
not the angel-faced mother nursing her rosy-cheeked baby
nor the apples on white cloth
nor the goldfish darting among aquarium bubbles
can you paint happiness Abidin
can you paint Cuba in midsummer 1961
master can you paint *Praise be praise be I saw the day I could die now*
and not be sorry
can you paint *What a pity what a pity I could have been born in*
Havana this morning
I saw a hand 150 kilometers east of Havana close to the sea
I saw a hand on a wall
the wall was an open song
the hand caressed the wall
the hand was six months old and stroked its mother's neck
the hand was seventeen years old and caressed Maria's breasts
its palm was calloused and smelled of the Caribbean
it was twenty and stroked the neck of its six-month-old son
the hand was twenty-five and had forgotten how to caress
the hand was thirty and I saw it on a wall near the sea 150
kilometers east of Havana caressing a wall
you draw hands Abidin those of our laborers and ironworkers
draw with charcoal the hand of the Cuban fisherman Nicolas
who on the wall of the shiny house he got from the cooperative
rediscovered caressing and won't forget it again
a big hand
a sea turtle of a hand

a hand that didn't believe it could caress an open wall
a hand that now believes in all joys
a sunny salty sacred hand
the hand of hopes that sprout green and sweeten with the speed
    of sugar cane in earth fertile as Fidel's words
one of the hands in Cuba in 1961 that plant houses like colorful
    cool trees and trees like very comfortable houses
one of the hands preparing to pour steel
the hand that makes songs of machine guns and machine guns
    of songs
the hand of freedom without lies
the hand Fidel shook
the hand that writes the word *freedom* with the first pencil and
    paper of its life
when they say the word *freedom* the Cubans' mouths water
as if they were slicing a honey of a melon
and the men's eyes gleam
and the girls melt when their lips touch the word *freedom*
and the old people draw from the well their sweetest memories
    and slowly sip them
can you paint happiness Abidin
can you paint freedom the kind without lies
night is falling in Paris
Notre Dame lit up like an orange lamp and went out
and in Paris all the stones old and new lit up like orange lamps
    and went out
I think of our crafts the business of poetry painting music and so on
I think and I know
a great river flows from the time the first human hand drew the
    first bison in the first cave
then all streams run into it with their new fish new water-grasses
    new tastes and it alone flows endlessly and never dries up
I've heard there's a chestnut tree in Paris
the first of the Paris chestnuts the granddaddy of them all
it came from Istanbul the hills of the Bosporus and settled in Paris

I don't know if it's still standing it would be about two hundred
   years old
I wish I could go shake its hand
I wish we could go lie in its shade the people who make the
   paper for this book who set its type who print its drawings
   those who sell this book in their stores who pay money and
   buy it who buy it and look at it and Abidin and me too plus
   the straw-blond trouble of my life

1961

UNTITLED

he was stone bronze plaster and paper anywhere from two
centimeters to seven meters
in all the city squares we were under his stone bronze
plaster and paper boots
in parks his stone bronze plaster and paper shadow darkened
our trees
his stone bronze plaster and paper mustache got in our soup
in restaurants
in our rooms we were under his stone bronze plaster and
paper eyes
he vanished one morning
   · his boots disappeared from our squares
his shadow from our trees
his mustache from our soup
his eyes from our rooms
and the weight of thousands of tons of stone bronze plaster
and paper was lifted off our backs

1961
Moscow

FALLING LEAVES

I've read about falling leaves in fifty thousand poems novels
   and so on
watched leaves falling in fifty thousand movies
seen leaves fall fifty thousand times
      fall drift and rot
felt their dead *shush shush* fifty thousand times
      underfoot in my hands on my fingertips
but I'm still touched by falling leaves
      especially those falling on boulevards
      especially chestnut leaves
      and if kids are around
      if it's sunny
      and I've got good news for friendship
especially if my heart doesn't ache
and I believe my love loves me
especially if it's a day I feel good about people
      I'm touched by falling leaves
especially those falling on boulevards
especially chestnut leaves

6 September 1961
Leipzig

WELCOME

welcome baby
it's your turn to live
they're laying for you chicken pox whooping cough smallpox
malaria TB heart disease cancer and so on
unemployment hunger and so on
train wrecks bus accidents plane crashes on-the-job injuries
earthquakes floods droughts and so on
heartbreak alcoholism and so on
nightsticks prison doors and so on
they're laying for you the atom bomb and so on
welcome baby
it's your turn to live
they're laying for you socialism communism and so on

10 September 1961
Leipzig

AUTOBIOGRAPHY

I was born in 1902
I never once went back to my birthplace
I don't like to turn back
at three I served as a pasha's grandson in Aleppo
at nineteen as a student at Moscow Communist University
at forty-nine I was back in Moscow as the Tcheka Party's guest
and I've been a poet since I was fourteen
some people know all about plants some about fish
                                        I know separation
some people know the names of the stars by heart
                                        I recite absences

I've slept in prisons and in grand hotels
I've known hunger even a hunger strike and there's almost no food
    I haven't tasted
at thirty they wanted to hang me
at forty-eight to give me the Peace Prize
                                    which they did
at thirty-six I covered four square meters of concrete in half a year
at fifty-nine I flew from Prague to Havana in eighteen hours
I never saw Lenin I stood watch at his coffin in '24
in '61 the tomb I visit is his books
they tried to tear me away from my party
                                it didn't work
nor was I crushed under falling idols
in '51 I sailed with a young friend into the teeth of death
in '52 I spent four months flat on my back with a broken heart
    waiting to die
I was jealous of the women I loved
I didn't envy Charlie Chaplin one bit
I deceived my women
I never talked behind my friends' backs
I drank but not every day
I earned my bread money honestly what happiness

out of embarrassment for others I lied
I lied so as not to hurt someone else
                  but I also lied for no reason at all
I've ridden in trains planes and cars
most people don't get the chance
I went to the opera
              most people haven't even heard of the opera
and since '21 I haven't gone to the places most people visit
         mosques churches temples synagogues sorcerers
         but I've had my coffee grounds read
my writings are published in thirty or forty languages
         in my Turkey in my Turkish they're banned
cancer hasn't caught up with me yet
and nothing says it will
I'll never be a prime minister or anything like that
and I wouldn't want such a life
nor did I go to war
or burrow in bomb shelters in the bottom of the night
and I never had to take to the road under diving planes
but I fell in love at almost sixty
in short comrades
even if today in Berlin I'm croaking of grief
              I can say I've lived like a human being
and who knows
              how much longer I'll live
              what else will happen to me

This autobiography was written
in East Berlin on 11 September 1961

THINGS I DIDN'T KNOW I LOVED

it's 1962 March 28th
I'm sitting by the window on the Prague-Berlin train
night is falling
I never knew I liked
night descending like a tired bird on a smoky wet plain
I don't like
comparing nightfall to a tired bird

I didn't know I loved the earth
can someone who hasn't worked the earth love it
I've never worked the earth
it must be my only Platonic love

and here I've loved rivers all this time
whether motionless like this they curl skirting the hills
European hills crowned with chateaus
or whether stretched out flat as far as the eye can see
I know you can't wash in the same river even once
I know the river will bring new lights you'll never see
I know we live slightly longer than a horse but not nearly as long
        as a crow
I know this has troubled people before
                        and will trouble those after me
I know all this has been said a thousand times before
                        and will be said after me

I didn't know I loved the sky
cloudy or clear
the blue vault Andrei studied on his back at Borodino
in prison I translated both volumes of *War and Peace* into Turkish
I hear voices
not from the blue vault but from the yard
the guards are beating someone again

I didn't know I loved trees
bare beeches near Moscow in Peredelkino
they come upon me in winter noble and modest
beeches are Russian the way poplars are Turkish
"the poplars of Izmir
losing their leaves...
they call me The Knife...
                              lover like a young tree...
I blow stately mansions sky-high"
in the Ilgaz woods in 1920 I tied an embroidered linen handkerchief
                              to a pine bough for luck

I never knew I loved roads
even the asphalt kind
Vera's behind the wheel we're driving from Moscow to the Crimea
                              Koktebele
                    formerly "Goktepé ili" in Turkish
the two of us inside a closed box
the world flows past on both sides distant and mute
I was never so close to anyone in my life
bandits stopped me on the red road between Bolu and Geredé
                    when I was eighteen
apart from my life I didn't have anything in the wagon they could take
and at eighteen our lives are what we value least
I've written this somewhere before
wading through a dark muddy street I'm going to the shadow play
Ramazan night
a paper lantern leading the way
maybe nothing like this ever happened
maybe I read it somewhere an eight-year-old boy
                              going to the shadow play
Ramazan night in Istanbul holding his grandfather's hand
   his grandfather has on a fez and is wearing the fur coat
      with a sable collar over his robe
   and there's a lantern in the servant's hand
   and I can't contain myself for joy

flowers come to mind for some reason
poppies cactuses jonquils
in the jonquil garden in Kadikoy Istanbul I kissed Marika
fresh almonds on her breath
I was seventeen
my heart on a swing touched the sky
I didn't know I loved flowers
friends sent me three red carnations in prison

I just remembered the stars
I love them too
whether I'm floored watching them from below
or whether I'm flying at their side

I have some questions for the cosmonauts
were the stars much bigger
did they look like huge jewels on black velvet
                              or apricots on orange
did you feel proud to get closer to the stars
I saw color photos of the cosmos in *Ogonek* magazine now don't
    be upset comrades but nonfigurative shall we say or abstract
    well some of them looked just like such paintings which is to
    say they were terribly figurative and concrete
my heart was in my mouth looking at them
they are our endless desire to grasp things
seeing them I could even think of death and not feel at all sad
I never knew I loved the cosmos

snow flashes in front of my eyes
both heavy wet steady snow and the dry whirling kind
I didn't know I liked snow

I never knew I loved the sun
even when setting cherry-red as now
in Istanbul too it sometimes sets in postcard colors
but you aren't about to paint it that way

I didn't know I loved the sea

                                    except the Sea of Azov

or how much

I didn't know I loved clouds
whether I'm under or up above them
whether they look like giants or shaggy white beasts

moonlight the falsest the most languid the most petit-bourgeois
strikes me
I like it

I didn't know I liked rain
whether it falls like a fine net or splatters against the glass my
    heart leaves me tangled up in a net or trapped inside a drop
    and takes off for uncharted countries I didn't know I loved
    rain but why did I suddenly discover all these passions sitting
    by the window on the Prague-Berlin train
is it because I lit my sixth cigarette
one alone could kill me
is it because I'm half dead from thinking about someone back in
    Moscow
her hair straw-blond eyelashes blue

the train plunges on through the pitch-black night
I never knew I liked the night pitch-black
sparks fly from the engine
I didn't know I loved sparks
I didn't know I loved so many things and I had to wait until sixty
    to find it out sitting by the window on the Prague-Berlin train
    watching the world disappear as if on a journey of no return

                                          19 April 1962
                                          Moscow

I STEPPED OUT OF MY THOUGHTS OF DEATH

I stepped out of my thoughts of death
and put on the June leaves of the boulevards
those of May after all were too young for me
a whole summer waits for me a city summer with its hot stones
    and asphalt
its ice-cold pop ice cream sweaty movie houses thick-voiced
    actors from the provinces
with its taxis that suddenly vanish on big soccer days
and its trees that turn to paper under the lights of the
    Hermitage garden
and maybe with Mexican songs or tom-toms from Ghana
and the poems I'll read on the balcony
and with your hair cut a little shorter
a city summer is waiting for me
I put on the June leaves of the boulevards
I stepped out of my thoughts of death

24 May 1962

I'M GETTING USED TO GROWING OLD

I'm getting used to growing old,
the hardest art in the world—
knocking on doors for the last time,
endless separation.
The hours run and run and run. . .
I want to understand at the cost of losing faith.
I tried to tell you something, and I couldn't.
The world tastes like an early morning cigarette:
death has sent me its loneliness first.
I envy those who don't even know they're growing old,
they're so buried in their work.

12 January 1963

BERLIN LETTERS

1
Berlin is bright and sunny.
March 8, 1963.
On the phone this morning
I forgot to wish you a happy holiday.
When I hear your voice, I forget the world.
Many happy returns, my beauty.

8 March 1963

2
In four days I'll be in Moscow.
This separation will also end, thank God, and I'll return.
I'll leave it behind like a rainy road.
New separations will follow,
I'll dip into new wells,
I'll take off for somewhere and come back.
I'll run, breathless, to new returns.
Then neither Berlin nor Tanganyika—
nowhere, I'll go nowhere.
I won't return—no boat, no train, no plane.
No letters will come from me, no telegrams.
And I won't call you on the phone.
You won't laugh softly at my voice
or get any more news from me—
you'll be left all alone.
In four days I'll be in Moscow.
Berlin is bright and sunny.
On the phone you said
it's spring in Moscow.
This separation will also end, thank God, and I'll return.
But inside me is the night of our great separation,

your pain of being without me,
your loneliness.
Loneliness—the tasteless bread of memories,
   their call to distance.
Maybe three months, maybe three years,
loneliness will shadow you.
In four days I'll be in Moscow.
On the phone you said
it's spring in Moscow.

8 April 1963

3
I'll be at your side in five hours.
In Berlin
            sunlight, birdsong
                  (it rained this morning),
                     streetcars,
                        and time
                           fill my hotel room.
Time doesn't move,
it's frozen solid.
You could hang it on a hanger
or cut it with a knife.
It's like being in prison,
            where time
                  is the cruelest guard.
I'll be at the airport in two hours.
In five, in your blue.
Freedom five hours away.
Statues of whoever invented airplanes
should grace the hotel rooms of all returns.

12 April 1963

MY FUNERAL

Will my funeral start out from our courtyard?
How will you get me down from the third floor?
The coffin won't fit in the elevator,
and the stairs are awfully narrow.

Maybe there'll be sun knee-deep in the yard, and pigeons,
maybe snow filled with the cries of children,
maybe rain with its wet asphalt.
And the trash cans will stand in the courtyard as always.

If, as is the custom here, I'm put in the truck face open,
a pigeon might drop something on my forehead: it's good luck.
Band or no band, the children will come up to me—
they're curious about the dead.

Our kitchen window will watch me leave.
Our balcony will see me off with the wash on the line.
In this yard I was happier than you'll ever know.
Neighbors, I wish you all long lives.

April 1963
Moscow

VERA

Come she said
Stay she said
Smile she said
Die she said

I came
I stayed
I smiled
I died

1963

NOTES

GIOCONDA AND SI-YA-U. Si-Ya-U: Hsiao San (b. 1896), Chinese revolutionary and man of letters. Hikmet met him in Moscow in 1922 and believed he had been executed in the bloody 1927 crackdown on Shanghai radicals after returning to China via Paris in 1924, when the Mona Lisa did in fact disappear from the Louvre. The two friends were reunited in Vienna in 1951 and traveled to Peking together in 1952. Translated into Chinese, this poem was later burned—along with Hsiao's own works—in the Cultural Revolution.

THE EPIC OF SHEIK BEDREDDIN. Bedreddin: Sheik Bedreddin (1359?–1420), Turkish scholar, mystic, and early socialist born in Simavné in the province of Edirné, educated in Konya and Cairo, and executed in Serrai in Macedonia for leading an uprising of Turkish, Greek, and Jewish peasants against Sultan Mehmet I. Ducasse (1400–1471): Byzantine historian who authored an important history of the Ottomans' rise. Mustafa: Turkish peasant from Karaburun crucified in Seljuk in 1417 for organizing a revolt against the Sultan in the provinces of Izmir and Aydin. Arabshah (1389–1450): Arabic scholar and poet. Ashikpashazadé (b. 1400): Ottoman historian. Neshri: fifteenth-century Ottoman historian. Idris of Bitlis (d. 1520): Ottoman statesman and historian who wrote a verse-history of the reigns of the first eight Ottoman sultans called *Eight Heavens*. Prince Musa: killed by his brother Mehmet in 1413 after ascending the throne in Edirné in 1411. Sultan Mehmet I: ruled from 1412 until his death in 1421, unifying the Ottoman Empire after numerous wars with his brothers. Prince Murad (1404–1451): Sultan Mehmet's son, who led his father's army against Mustafa in 1416 and became Sultan Murad II in 1421. Bayezid Pasha (d. 1421): Sultan Mehmet's vizier and commander of the army sent against Mustafa. Kemal: Jewish peasant hanged in Manisa in 1417 for preaching Bedreddin's philosophy there. Mevlana Haydar: Persian scholar reported to have sentenced Bedreddin to death. Shekerullah bin Shehabeddin: Ottoman historian.

ON DEATH AGAIN. Piraye: Hatice Zekiye Pirayende, Hikmet's third wife.

ISTANBUL HOUSE OF DETENTION. Sinan (1489–1588): Ottoman architect. Yunus Emré (1250–1320): Turkish folk poet. Sakarya: river in central Anatolia and the site of a major battle in the Turkish War of Independence.

LETTERS FROM CHANKIRI PRISON. Ghazali (d. 1534): Ottoman poet.

9–10 P.M. POEMS. The title derives from the hour before lights out in prison, when Hikmet promised his wife to think and write only of her.

RUBAIYAT. In December 1945 Hikmet wrote his wife, "I'm going to try something that's never been done in Western or Eastern literature—put dialectical materialism into the rubaiyat form." The technical issue of adapting a traditional form to new content preoccupied him from the start. In a letter to his stepson, Memet Fuat, he suggests the original form served as a model: "True poets, those who have mastered their art, never write without some kind of measure or rhyme—even though they may deny it—because if they did, they'd be writing prose. In writing quatrains, rhyme is important, because rubaiyat—even the most philosophical or lyrical—are a species of polemical, didactic weapons in poetry. They must be easily memorized; they must be economically phrased. The classical rhyme scheme [aaba] makes all that possible. But sometimes a modern use of rhyme may be substituted for the classical scheme." In his first few rubaiyat, he reports, he worked to retain the classical form as a sort of warm-up exercise; subsequently, he played variations on it to accommodate his new content. Rumi: Jelaluddin Rumi (1207–1273), Sufi mystic poet who founded in Turkey the order of whirling dervishes. Khayyam: Omar Khayyam, twelfth-century Persian poet. Yahya Kemal (1884-1958): Turkish poet who declined to sign a petition demanding Hikmet's release from prison.

ON IBRAHIM BALABAN'S PAINTING "SPRING." Ibrahim Balaban (b. 1921): Turkish artist Hikmet introduced to painting in prison.

TO LYDIA IVANNA. Kostya: Konstantin Simonov (b. 1915), Russian poet. Memet: Hikmet's son, born in 1951.

TO SAMET VURGUN. Samet Vurgun (1906-1956), Azerbaijani poet.

LETTER FROM ISTANBUL. Munevver: Munevver Andaç, Hikmet's fourth wife, who emigrated to Paris and translated his work into French.

IN THE SNOWY NIGHT WOODS. Bierut: Boleslaw Bierut, the first president of Poland (1947-1956). Widely regarded as a Soviet puppet, he was nevertheless rumored to have been poisoned in the Kremlin during a state visit to the former USSR. Bayramoghlu: early Azerbaijani Communist killed in Baku in 1919, presumably by White Russians in the civil war that followed the Bolshevik Revolution but possibly by the Red Army, which history now shows engaged even then in ethnic-cleansing operations against Turkish-speaking populations. The mysterious deaths of these "good Communists" may have preyed on Hikmet's mind, for KGB files opened in 1994 reveal that Hikmet was a marked man in the Soviet Union from the start. His telephone was routinely bugged, the man he considered his closest friend informed against him, and the secret police first tried to enlist his driver to stage a fatal car accident and later plotted with the Bulgarian government to poison him.

SOME MEMORIES. Nezval: Vitezslav Nezval (1900-1958), Czech poet.

THIRTY YEARS AGO. Komsomol: Communist Youth Organization.

THE CUCUMBER. Ekber Babayev: Russian translator, editor, and critic.

TO VERA. Vera: Vera Tulyakova, Hikmet's fifth wife, who lived in Moscow and published a memoir of their years together.

STRAW-BLOND. Sait Faik (1906-1954): Turkish fiction writer. Abidin: Abidin Dino (1913-1993), Turkish artist who illustrated many of Hikmet's books. Avni: Avni Arbaş (b. 1919), Turkish artist. Levni (d. 1732): Ottoman miniaturist